KU-002-789

The All Colour Book of
Family Meals

Audrey Ellis

TREASURE PRESS

Notes
All recipes serve 4 people unless otherwise stated
Plain flour and granulated sugar are used unless otherwise stated
All eggs are standard
Ovens should be preheated to the specified temperature

Contents

Part One

Part Two

First published at All Colour Budget Cookery
Book by Sundial Publications Limited
This edition published by Treasure Press
59 Grosvenor Street
London W1

© 1977 Hennerwood Publications Limited

ISBN 0 907407 03 X

Printed in Hong Kong

Good shopping sense

Seven golden rules: Rule 1

Always make a shopping list before setting out (except for the odd small purchase).

Plan the family's menus for the next few days before compiling your list for a big shopping spree. It takes so little time and makes the expedition to the shops much more worth while. Jotting down the items you need for the meals you have planned saves time at the shops and ensures that you will not have to rush out again to buy some essential item from the expensive corner shop.

Train yourself and the rest of the family to use a memo board, prominently displayed in the kitchen, to note down when any particular item runs low. If you always eat toast for breakfast and never have cause to check the contents of the breakfast cereal packets, put the onus on the cereal eaters.

In these days when you buy large quantities at a time in self-service stores, you may find it hard to estimate how much you are spending until you are asked for the total amount. Sometimes this can be an unpleasant shock. Admittedly it takes a little trouble to note down the cost of each item as you put it in your basket or trolley, but afterwards you will have a complete record of how the money was spent.

Stick to your shopping list as far as possible but do not be fanatical about it. Try to avoid being tempted by luxury goods you know you cannot afford, and which would mean re-thinking your menus. On the other hand, develop your powers of judgement. When you see an item you would normally consider in the luxury class on sale in peak condition and at a price that makes it almost a bargain, decide quickly whether to make the purchase. For instance, if you had intended to make a beef stew with fresh tomatoes and you then notice that beautiful avocados are unusually low in price, you must decide whether you can offer a starter made with avocado and replace the fresh tomatoes in the beef stew with something cheaper. This is not a skill easily or quickly acquired, but it does come with time and patience and is worth the effort if you want to make the most of a limited housekeeping budget.

It is essential to have a sturdy, safe shopping basket or bag. One sometimes sees the sad evidence of an overweighted carrier in the form of a broken bottle or carton of smashed eggs on the pavement.

Rule 2

Learn what to look for when buying canned and packaged foods. Sometimes inexperienced shoppers do not notice what the contents of a pack weigh and imagine, for instance, that all jam jars hold the same amount of jam. In fact, pack contents are by law very plainly displayed on their labels. One mystifying exception is canned milk. Both evaporated and condensed milks are described by the reconstituted quantity of natural strength milk they will provide.

Canned fruit may be of average or choice quality, and it may be canned in light or heavy syrup. It is always preferable to buy a couple of different canned fruits to mix with prepared fresh fruits rather than the product described on the can as 'fruit salad' or 'fruit cocktail'. One has to pay for the slicing, dicing and mixing of different fruits.

Canned condensed soups provide an equivalent amount of soup of the same strength as an ordinary can of soup twice the size. All packs of biscuits are marked with the weight they contain, and these weights vary. Be vigilant and always check the pack contents when you estimate whether biscuits are cheap or expensive.

Biscuit packs which are not date marked may prove disappointing when opened at home if the biscuits are stale and soft. It really pays to shop at a store where all the food, even if not date marked, is certain to be in peak condition.

Besides care in choosing canned goods, a certain amount of expertise is needed with packaged dry goods. Make sure your packs are perfect. This really applies to all wrapped goods where the seal is all important to ensure freshness. Bread products are a good example because if air can enter the pack through a tear in the wrapping, the bread will not be as fresh as it should be. If wrapping has been commercially perforated then obviously this has been done to keep the product in the best condition possible. Cakes and dairy products are almost always date marked and if you shop late on a Saturday you can sometimes take advantage of these items being offered at a reduced price, because they would overrun the date mark by the following Monday. But the disadvantage of this is that the selection of perishable goods may well be limited because many of them may be sold out.

Rule 3

Plan carefully where to shop. If you have plenty of time to spare for shopping, and it is a job you really enjoy, visit a number of stores and compare prices. Sometimes there is a 'loss leader' offered to induce a housewife to do all her shopping in one particular store, just to acquire the bargain offer of the week. But ask yourself whether this is done because the other produce in the store is not of the high quality or wide choice you would like to see. You may be better off, especially if you have no time to carry out your own market survey every week, to stick to favourite stores where value is always good and produce always reliable.

We have to get used to buying larger amounts and giving up the old habit of a quick foray round the shops every day, now generally accepted as being a poor use of time. The small corner shop which can be visited in a few minutes for just one forgotten item, or for a few items every day, is almost bound to charge more for its personal service than the big stores.

Note on a memo board items which are running low.

The sad evidence of an overweighted carrier bag

HINTS ON SUGAR

1. If you are disappointed on opening canned fruit to find that the syrup is too light in strength, you can easily adjust it to your requirements. Drain the syrup and boil it until it reduces in quantity to make a heavier syrup, or heat it with added sugar and when this has dissolved boil it for a few minutes until sufficiently concentrated. In both these cases cool before pouring over the fruit.
2. If syrup from canned fruit is too heavy in strength, drain it and stir in sufficient water and a few drops of lemon juice to give the required concentration.
3. Soft light brown and dark brown sugars and demerara sugar tend to form a solid block in the pack when stored for more than a few weeks. Directions are usually given on the pack how to soften the sugar if this happens but, in general, the best way to soften the finer sugars is to empty the pack into a basin and put a damp cloth across the top of the basin overnight. To soften demerara sugar, empty the pack into an ovenproof basin and warm it in the oven.
4. If members of the family use a large quantity of sugar to sweeten drinks, it is cheaper to buy sweetening tablets and insist that they are used to replace all or some of the sugar.

HINTS ON CREAM AND BUTTER

1. Substitute your own home-made pastry cream for fresh cream. Layered with jam in a victoria sandwich, or as a filling for éclairs, it costs less and keeps well in an airtight container for a week in the refrigerator or for months in the freezer.
2. Crème chantilly, which is made by folding stiffly whisked egg whites into sweetened and vanilla-flavoured whipped cream costs less to serve than whipped cream alone. This gives it a pleasant light texture and very much increases the bulk.
3. To economize on butter, substitute oil for frying, margarine for creaming and savoury sandwiches and reserve the luxury of butter for spreading bread, crispbreads or toast.
4. If your family is heavy handed with butter, extend it. Beat 225 g/8 oz butter until it is soft, then gradually beat in 4 × 15 ml spoons/4 tablespoons hot water. Or you could use boiling milk. The bulk is much increased and the butter can be spread more thinly even when cold.

Rule 4

Appraise the quality of fresh foods with a knowledgeable eye.

Fruit and vegetables vary in price in ways many housewives find mystifying. The system of marking by Class, according to quality, is not always honoured, and it is much better to be able to select unerringly Class I produce without being guided by the shopkeeper.

Where you can choose your own fruit individually, or examine every item in a netted pack, no-one else is to blame if you bring home a shrivelled orange, or a pear with a bruised spot on it. You can judge the juiciness of a citrus fruit by its weight (which should be heavy for its size if the fruit is juicy), or assess from the colour of its skin whether a pear is nearly ripe, verging on overripe, or that it must be kept in a warm place for at least a week before it will be eatable. If an assistant selects and weighs up fruit or vegetables, it is only natural that a few less-than-perfect specimens will find their way into your brown paper bag!

Vegetables such as Brussels sprouts should have been carefully trimmed or you will be paying for a lot of wastage. This also applies to vegetables such as celery and leeks. You may not always be charged by weight but it is disappointing when buying what appears at a quick glance to be a beautiful head of celery, if you find that a number of outer stalks have to be trimmed away before you get to those which are edible. Keep your eyes open and especially concentrate on shopping for fresh foods.

Fish is often tricky to buy because if it comes fresh from the fishmonger's slab you can never be sure of its history.

Has it been frozen at sea, subsequently defrosted and then frozen again before it took its place as part of a well arranged display? Almost everyone has had the experience of arriving home with a purchase of fish wrapped in clean white paper which smells suspicious as soon as it is unwrapped. Frozen fish from a reputable source often smells fresher when removed from its pack. It is also completely trimmed of waste, and this accounts for a considerable part of the cost. Salmon, which is always expensive, is often sold as fresh fish when in fact it is frequently frozen Canadian salmon defrosted. In general, fresh fish should be firm, with silvery scales and bright eyes. The slightest hint of an ammoniac aroma is a danger signal.

One must be particularly careful about the freshness of shellfish sold 'in the shell'. For instance, mussels which fail to open and close again when the shell is sharply tapped are already dead and not fit to use. If you buy them in this way you will probably find that a few have to be discarded. If it is more than a few you have made a bad buy.

Meat other than beef is usually easy to judge by its appearance. Veal, lamb and pork which do not require long hanging to tenderize and develop a mature flavour, are best when the fat is white or pale cream, and the flesh pink in colour. Make sure that lamb and pork do not have too high a proportion of fat. Pork chops sold with the rind on may seem relatively inexpensive compared with those which are sold neatly trimmed, but remember you will have to trim off the rind and some of the fat before cooking them. This is not so wasteful if you carefully render out the fat and make use of it later.

Beef requires at least ten days hanging to become really tender. The fat may then appear almost yellow in colour and the lean meat rather dry and dark. It is not as attractive as beef which is bright red, dripping with blood, and with a white fat, but if you buy it in this latter condition be sure to ask the butcher whether it has been properly hung. If it proves unexpectedly tough when carefully cooked, you have a legitimate complaint. Also steer clear of the store which sells packed cuts of meat containing fatty pieces hidden beneath an attractive cut laid on top of them. This applies to bacon and cooked meats too, of course.

Nowadays dairy foods and margarine are usually displayed in a refrigerated cabinet. Cheese is often shrink wrapped and this makes it hard to appraise, but when it is labelled 'mild' or 'mature' you can judge that the latter will have a fuller flavour. Continental soft or crusted cheeses may feel firm to fingertip pressure through the wrap but when returned to room temperature they are in fact just ready to eat. Here you really must trust the store not to offer immature or overripe cheeses.

Fresh and not-so-fresh produce

Cabbage is excellent in casseroles and salads

HINTS ON CABBAGE

1. This leafy vegetable appears more often on the table than any other. It is available in many forms, including the white drumhead, curly green savoy and red cabbage. The base and core of the cut cabbage are heavy and must be discarded. Be sure to check that the base of the cabbage is good to avoid wasting money, especially if some outer leaves have been stripped off because they have begun to decay.
2. Cooking in a closed casserole in the oven saves heat when the oven is in use, and conserves all the nutritional value which is often wasted when boiling in too much water. For example, layer sliced and washed white cabbage with salt, pepper, caraway seeds and a little margarine. Cover and oven bake it in a casserole.
3. When salads are expensive, washed and finely shredded green cabbage has a nutty flavour and combined with a dressing makes an excellent alternative.
4. Red cabbage requires long slow cooking and it is an economy to layer it in a greased casserole (so that it requires no fatty bacon on the base of a pan placed on the hob to prevent it from burning) and use up oven heat that would otherwise be wasted. It has the advantage that it is almost impossible to overcook it by this method.

Rule 5

Stock up wisely for your family's needs. This means resisting the temptation to buy economy foods no-one really likes. You will waste more in the end by throwing away unconsumed portions and being forced to provide something extra because everyone is still hungry. Certain foods are economical, and it is worth studying new recipes to use them in interesting ways. But, if they really are far down on the list of favourites, no matter how you disguise them they may be wasted in the end. On the other hand, if there are staple foods you continually use in large quantities, there is no risk attached to buying them in bulk.

It is a frequent temptation to buy large quantities of foods at cheaper prices which you know your family will enjoy, but which will throw your budget out of gear. If you can be firm with yourself and resist spending it until you see a real bargain, it really is economical to keep a small sum of money in reserve for special purchases.

Experience teaches discretion; supplies of a useful product which result in overstocking to the extent of exceeding your requirements for many months ahead may not be such a good idea. The food may deteriorate if it is stored in unsuitable conditions because you really have nowhere else to put it. Even a sack of potatoes will start sprouting if stored for long in a cupboard.

Rule 6

Arrange storage space to keep food accessible and in peak condition. This means that you need to have a system in order to bring packs and cans forward in rotation. It is so easy to place a pack at the back of the shelf, overlook it and continue to put new packs in front of it. You will always be using up fresh stock while the food in the neglected pack is becoming stale, and even with dry goods this does eventually lead to deterioration of quality. In fact, you could lose all the profit you have gained by careful shopping if one pack has to be thrown away. Make it a rule to put new food supplies at the back of the shelf and bring existing supplies forward every time you put away your shopping.

It is important to know how different foods require to be stored:

Green vegetables soon shrivel and go yellow if stored in the dark without protection from dry air. It is worth storing them in closed polythene bags in the refrigerator along with delicate salad vegetables, for which a special drawer is usually provided at the bottom. This is not near the ice-making compartment and is therefore not cold enough to overchill green vegetables and salads. Fully prepared vegetables keep well in the refrigerator for up to a week in a closed polythene pack. To save space and preparation time when cooking, it is a good idea to prepare them before storage. Who wants to waste refrigerator space on outer leaves and stalks which will only have to be thrown away later?

Root vegetables are bulky, and are often stored in a cupboard because there is rarely enough room in the refrigerator. All too often they are put away in the brown paper bags in which they were bought. These bags give no protection to the vegetables against drying out and shrivelling in warm, dry air. They can be sealed in polythene bags although this has its dangers unless the contents of each bag are examined frequently; if there is any hint of spoilage it will soon spread to all the vegetables in the bag. Damage from moulds spreads very quickly, which is why items like tomatoes, apples and pears should each be separately wrapped in paper for long storage, or spread out on racks so that they do not touch. Since tomatoes are really fruit, the maturing process continues for some time before spoilage begins, but vegetables begin to deteriorate immediately they are harvested.

Deterioration in soft berry fruits, as in vegetables, begins quickly, often within hours, and it is much better to turn them out of the punnet in which they were purchased into another container, so that you can remove any damaged specimens from the bottom of the pack. The refrigerator is really the only safe storage space for soft berry fruits. Hard-skinned fruits, including plums, cranberries and gooseberries, are not such delicate items. All fruits which require further ripening, especially bananas and peaches, are better decoratively arranged in a fruit bowl or basket and left exposed to warm air to hasten the process.

Meat, which is such an expensive item, requires very careful storage. The rule is, keep it covered but not sealed. This is easily done by putting the meat on a plate, slipping the plate into a polythene bag, and folding the open end underneath it without actually sealing the bag. Never store cooked and raw meat together in the same pack.

Raw meat cannot be safely kept longer than three to five days in the refrigerator and the larger the proportion of cut surfaces, the shorter the time. Large joints will keep the longest, and minced meat the shortest time.

Oven-ready chilled poultry, in a sealed pack, is better left sealed because the flesh tends to dry out and the delicate flavour is adversely affected by picking up flavours from other items in the refrigerator.

Raw fish has a strong aroma and should be kept fully sealed to protect other food which easily picks up a 'fishy' flavour. It is extremely perishable and should not be kept for longer than three days in the refrigerator. Raw pork and beef sausages should be treated as for poultry.

Smoked sausages, bacon and smoked fish should be packed in a closed wrap. They store well for twice as long as the raw product.

All dairy foods, eggs and fats should be stored in the special refrigerator door compartments designed for them, where the atmosphere is not too cold. However, families who use up their supplies within a week need not refrigerate them at all.

The question of storing leftovers is a vexed one. Common sense is the only reliable guide, since the ingredients and the manner in which they were cooked decide the length of time it is safe to store them. Always keep them covered, placed either in the refrigerator, or on a cool larder shelf. For example, a small amount of meat and vegetable stew would be better in the refrigerator but a wedge of steamed sponge pudding could be placed on any cool airy shelf to await reheating and serving.

Rule 7

Exploit freezer storage space, or the frozen food storage compartment of your refrigerator. Food which is frozen can be stored for a much longer time than unfrozen food because it is kept at a very low temperature.

Wraps which would give sufficient protection under normal conditions are not proof against the extremely cold dry air inside a freezer. Unless the pack is completely airtight and made of moisture-vapour-proof material, very cold air can actually penetrate it, draw moisture out of the food and dehydrate it. It then passes back through the pack into the cabinet, producing more frost. Seriously affected food, especially meat, actually shows greyish patches called freezer burn.

Sometimes packs are completely proof against invasion but leave unnecessary air spaces within themselves. The food will then dehydrate and form frost crystals inside the pack. Do be sure that your packs are perfectly airtight, made of a freezer-proof material, and that all air spaces are eliminated except for those required for the slight expansion of the water content of food as it freezes.

Label and date mark food carefully if it is not already in a labelled and marked commercial pack. This will help you to use up your frozen stock in rotation because, just as with cupboard storage, some packs tend to be neglected and not brought forward in their turn.

The temperature inside the freezer should be maintained constantly just below freezing point ($-18°C$, $0°F$). Recommended storage times, which may vary from as short a period as one month, to long periods up to a year, are designed to give guidance on peak quality in texture and flavour when the food is defrosted, although properly packed food will remain edible for considerably longer.

The safety rule in packing is to avoid contamination by using absolutely clean hands, utensils and wraps, blanching to halt enzyme activity in vegetables if advised, and preparing only perfect produce. The three 'C's are important; cool food quickly – keep it clean – keep it covered.

If you rely on a frozen food storage compartment in your refrigerator, the temperature it maintains will only keep frozen food for the time indicated by the star rating. Buying in bulk is not practical unless you wish to devote the whole of your storage space to a few frequently used items. A supply of ice cubes and a few packs of ready-prepared frozen meals for emergencies would be invaluable assets in this limited storage space.

Exploit storage space to the full, dividing food according to the type of storage that suits it best.

Good catering sense

Six golden rules: Rule 1

Learn the secrets of good nutrition. Most of us tend naturally to eat the foods we enjoy and – with the exception of the diet-conscious or the health food enthusiast – do not pause to consider what these foods are doing for us, or in some cases, to us! It is food that gives us the energy we need for every waking activity. Sensible eating and drinking are therefore necessary for good health and vitality and it is important that family meal planning should be influenced not only by considerations of budget but also by a thorough understanding of food values and essential nutrients.

Energy nutrients

Protein, fats and carbohydrates are the three main body 'fuels', and without regular supply of these our 'engine' would not function effectively. The energy produced from the burning-up of these fuels is measured in calories – a term familiar to weight-watchers who know that surplus calories not needed for energy are converted into fat stored under the skin to act as a fuel 'reserve'. It is these reserves that are burnt up during dieting, and this can be a slow and painful process if you are re-educating taste buds crying out for forbidden sweet or fatty foods. Overweight is a threat to health, and a great deal better prevented than cured; another good reason for a positive approach to sensible meal planning.

PROTEIN: This is the body-builder, helping to form and maintain strong tissues and muscles – and therefore particularly vital for growing children. Protein is found in meat, fish, eggs, cheese, milk, poultry, beans, peas and bread.

FATS: These store heat and energy and are found mainly in animal foods, such as butter, cream, milk, eggs and cheese.

CARBOHYDRATES: These are sources of quick energy, contained in starches and sugar. They are found in foods of vegetable origin, such as rice, flour, bread, oats, breakfast cereals and pasta. These are the foods we can best do without when trying to lose weight.

Protective nutrients

Several minerals are vital to the growth and upkeep of a healthy body, and most of them are found in sufficient quantities for our needs in the foods we eat every day. Two, however, are particularly vital to our well-being – calcium and iron – and special care must be taken to see that foods containing these are eaten regularly.

CALCIUM: Essential for the care and repair of bones and teeth. This is found mainly in milk, cheese, eggs and bread.

IRON: Used for the formation of red blood corpuscles. Found in most animal foods, especially liver, meat, egg yolk, watercress and spinach. Other green vegetables are essential too because they contain Vitamin C and the roughage and bulk essential to our digestive processes.

VITAMINS: The four vitamins, A, B, C and D, are well distributed in a diet based on all the foods mentioned above, so few people need to take vitamin pills in addition unless a doctor specifically advises it.

HINTS ON EGGS

1. When breaking a number of eggs, have ready a bowl and a cup. Break each egg into the cup first to make sure it is fresh. If they are broken one after another into a large bowl, one which is not fresh would contaminate all the others.
2. To ensure that egg whites are whisked stiffly enough for meringues etc. tilt the bowl of whisked egg white and shake gently. If the contents slide at all, they are not ready.
3. To whisk egg whites for soufflés and desserts, whisk only until they stand in peaks, look shiny and cling to the whisk or beaters. If overwhisked until the whites look 'dry' they will not incorporate easily and may give a grainy texture to the finished dessert.
4. To prevent home-made meringue from 'weeping', add a pinch of cream of tartar to the sugar and bake on a sheet of non-stick vegetable parchment. This makes sure that the meringue sets firm and dry and can easily be removed after baking.
5. Hard-boiled eggs sometimes show a line of discoloration round the yolks. To prevent this cover the hot, drained eggs with cold water and allow to stand for 5 minutes before shelling them. Then tap the eggs gently all over against a hard surface until the shell is covered in cracks. Remove it together with the inner skin.

HINTS ON FRUIT

1. Never throw away orange or lemon halves which have been squeezed, without grating off the zest. This is useful to add flavour to many sweet and savoury dishes and stores well in small polythene containers. It is easier to grate the zest before cutting and squeezing the fruit.
2. If you are too busy to grate orange zest, remove the rind in thin slivers, place on a baking tray and dry slowly in the oven as it cools down after use. It may require to be returned several times to the oven. Snip it up finely and keep in an airtight container to use as flavouring.
3. To peel peaches and grapes easily for delicate desserts, plunge them first into very hot water for one minute, then into cold water. The skin will then slip off easily.
4. To stone cherries and grapes, use a new hair pin, sterilized by standing it in boiling water until it becomes cool. Insert the rounded end of the hairpin into the cherry or grape, hook it round the stone or pips and pull out quickly. Do this over a basin to catch any juice which may spurt out.

Above: Foods rich in fats
Centre: Foods rich in
proteins
Below: Foods rich in
calcium

Above: Foods rich in
carbohydrates
Below: Foods rich in iron

Rule 2

Know how to interpret recipes so that you won't make mistakes which could result in the failure of a dish and wastage of the ingredients.

INGREDIENTS: A good recipe should tell you exactly what ingredients you are going to need, how to prepare them, and how to cook them to achieve a satisfactory result. A good cook, whether experienced or a beginner, should always check through the list to make sure they are all in the store cupboard before she starts work – otherwise it is all too easy for a recipe to fail for the lack of some vital item. Ingredients in this book are listed in order of use, together with the exact quantity required unless this may vary. Occasionally a particular ingredient, say butter, is used in two parts while preparing a dish – once to sauté vegetables and later to dot over the top of the dish before it is finished under the grill. In this case it is usually listed once, giving the total quantity needed for both stages, and the amount to be used at the sauté stage is then stated in the method.

Ingredients are also clearly described so there is no confusion between items that can be used either fresh or dried – for example breadcrumbs or herbs – which could affect the finished dish. Use fresh unless dried are specified.

METHOD: My recipes are given in simple, easy-to-follow terms, describing how to prepare the food for cooking, what actual form of cooking should be used, and how the dish should be served. Remember always to read the recipe right through to make sure that as well as the necessary ingredients, you also have the utensils – bowls, spoons, whisks, etc. – that you are going to need. Cooking is simpler and more enjoyable if you get into the habit of laying out all equipment on your work surface before you begin, rather than scrabbling with floury hands for a measuring spoon.

As well as telling you what to do, each recipe also gives the quantity it will serve, unless it is to serve four people, the cooking time and the oven temperature if necessary. These recipes have been tested and tasted by experts, but it is essential to follow them carefully if you are to achieve perfect results. Take care when weighing or measuring out the given quantities of each ingredient, as even a small alteration or mistake can have a surprising effect on the finished dish. An accurate set of scales, measuring spoons and graduated measuring cups for liquid ingredients are sensible investments that will pay dividends in good results. It is also important to use the right size of frying pan, saucepan or baking dish if specified; many a good cake has been ruined through being cooked in a deep tin when the recipe called for a wider shallow one. If the recipe calls for the cooking utensil to be covered, do not ignore this direction because it often greatly affects the finished dish.

TIMING IS IMPORTANT: A timer or oven alarm clock is a great help to accurate timing. Use it to remind you when to lower the oven heat or baste the joint, or to let you know that cooking time is up.

ADVANCE PREPARATION: Having assembled your ingredients, it is a good idea to prepare each of them as far as possible before you start to mix them – chopping, grating, peeling, melting or whatever is appropriate. This is the trick that makes television cookery appear so effortless – the little bowl of chopped onion, and another of green peppers waiting to be tipped into the measured amount of butter sizzling in the pan – but it is well worth doing in your own kitchen even if you have no audience!

Puréeing cucumber for soup

Rule 3

Learn to understand cookery terms and techniques. Certain cookery terms ought to be fully understood in order to prevent expensive errors. Cooking is, at its simplest, the application of heat to food in order to make it both palatable and appetizing. But different methods of cooking can give equally different textures and flavours to the same foods. Your choice of method will, of course, depend mainly on the recipe, and the type of cooker and equipment you have available. Just a few commonly used terms are confusing and require some explanation.

Blanch to pour boiling water over the food to loosen the skins of some foods such as tomatoes. Blanching may also be done by covering food in cold water and bringing to the boil before straining off the water. Blanching vegetables for freezing is done by immersing them in fast boiling water for a carefully calculated length of time.

Braise to brown in a small amount of very hot fat and then simmer slowly on a bed of vegetables with a small amount of liquid in a covered dish.

Brown to cook quickly on all sides in hot fat to seal in the juices of meat; or to finish a cooked dish by putting it under the grill or in a hot oven to crisp and colour the surface.

Casserole to cook meat or vegetables with some liquid slowly in a covered dish at a low temperature in the oven or on top of the stove.

Devil to coat with hot seasoning, usually before frying, grilling or barbecuing.

Flame to ignite a liqueur or other spirit poured over food after cooking.

Par-boil to boil only until partially cooked, usually finishing cooking by another method.

Parcel-cook to enclose food completely in foil or several layers of greaseproof paper, thus sealing in and retaining moisture. The parcel is then placed in a baking tray in the oven.

Whipping egg whites with a balloon whisk

Poach to cook gently in simmering liquid.

Pot-roast to cook meat or vegetables in a covered pan with a small amount of liquid.

Reduce to boil rapidly, uncovered, to get rid of excess water and thus concentrate the flavour.

Sauté to fry in a small amount of fat, turning constantly.

Simmer to cook in liquid just below boiling point.

Stew to cook food in a large proportion of liquid at simmering point, in a covered pan, on the stove or in the oven.

Even simple techniques are not always understood and carried out correctly. Here are some definitions of everyday cookery processes:

Baste to moisten food with melted fat to prevent it drying while it cooks.

Beat to make ingredients smooth, using a spoon, whisk or mixer.

Blend to mix together different ingredients OR to prepare food in an electric blender.

Chop to cut food into small pieces.

Coat to cover food completely with flour, beaten egg and crumbs, etc.

Cool to allow hot food to return to room temperature.

Cream to beat food to a creamy consistency with a fork or mixer.

Dice to cut food, usually vegetables, into small cubes.

Dredge to cover food with a dry substance, such as flour or icing sugar.

Grate to use a hand grater to reduce food to coarse, medium or fine particles.

Knead to work mixture, such as dough, by hand, pulling and folding over.

Liquidize to reduce moist foods to a smooth liquid in an electric blender.

Marinate to leave food in a flavoured mixture to absorb the flavour or become tender.

Mince to produce very small particles of food, using a hand mincer or electric grinder.

Purée to put food through a sieve or blender to produce a thick smooth mixture.

Score to cut shallow slits in surface of food, usually meat, before cooking, to increase tenderness or to prevent fat from curling over.

Shred to cut food into fine lengths, using a knife or hand or electric shredder.

Sieve to pass food through a sieve to produce a fine consistency, removing pips, skin etc.

Sift to shake dry ingredients through a sieve to prevent lumps and incorporate air for lightness.

Steep to stand food in a hot liquid to extract flavour or colour.

Toss to mix ingredients lightly, by a lifting motion, for example, lettuce and French dressing.

Whip to beat ingredients with a whisk, rotary beater or electric mixer.

Rule 4

Work out well-balanced meals with plenty of variety. If you are giving a dinner party, you will be prepared to spend time and thought in planning the meal beforehand, and working out what dishes will combine or contrast effectively in terms of flavour, texture and colour, as well as considering the taste and appetites of your guests! When it comes to everyday eating, however, you are less likely to do much in the way of preplanning, even though the health and well-being of your family depends to a great extent on the meals you provide. Planning the meals for two or three days ahead at the same time helps to ensure a balanced diet, and can also be economical in time.

It is helpful to think of food as divided into four main groups:

BREAD AND CEREALS: flour, rice, pasta, breakfast cereals.

DAIRY PRODUCTS: milk, butter, cheese, cream, yogurt.

FRUITS AND VEGETABLES: potatoes, root vegetables, pulses, peas, beans, bananas, green vegetables, citrus and soft fruits, tomatoes.

ANIMAL FOODS: meat, offal, fish, poultry, eggs.

An easy rule is to serve at least one and preferably two foods from each group every day. It is sensible to choose the main dish of the main meal first, as this is the most important and usually the most expensive item on the shopping list, and will affect the choice of accompanying dishes and courses. The size of helpings is obviously governed by individual appetites, but it is often better to serve second helpings than to pile a daunting amount of food on to each plate. Remember that just as appetites will vary between, say, energetic teenagers and their grandparents so, too, do calorie requirements. If already a satisfactory weight, most women can keep their weight steady on about 2,000 calories a day, and men on about 2,500, whereas a sixteen-year-old boy will need up to 3,000 calories per day. A word of warning – you only have to clock up 3,500 calories surplus to your body's needs to put on an extra half kilo or one pound!

Cost will probably be a major consideration in meal planning. Fortunately it is still possible to be budget-wise without being food-foolish and skimping on essential nourishment – the cheaper cuts of meat have exactly the same protein value as prime steak. Here again, it is worth planning to transform unglamorous scrag end of lamb into a glorious casserole dish, by adding herbs and colourful vegetables.

Rule 5

Plan regular sessions for batch cooking. There is usually one morning or afternoon in the week, or it may be an evening, when you can devote a couple of hours to cooking in quantity.

Best of all is a baking session, and now that fuel costs have to be carefully checked, you will be more eager than ever to fill the oven each time you use it. In a couple of hours you can produce a great assortment of pasties, tartlets, flans and cheese straws. Or you may prefer to make layer cakes, biscuits and scones.

If you are a freezer owner, you will often reserve this time for cooking two main dishes in king-size quantities. Serve one portion of the first main dish and freeze down two future meals. Refrigerate one portion of the second main dish to serve the next day and freeze the rest.

Some recipes have a number of variations on the basic theme. For instance, a simple biscuit dough may be capable of producing two or three different flavours. You could make up twice the quantity of creamed mixture for Peanut biscuits and divide this in half. Fold in the flour with the peanuts and raisins to one part, and add chocolate dots or crushed butterscotch sweets with the flour to the other half. In less than an hour you will have about a hundred assorted biscuits to keep the family happy.

HINTS ON CHEESE

1. To prevent the surface of cut cheese from becoming oily, cover closely with plastic cling wrap, seal and store near the bottom of the refrigerator. To prevent ripe, soft-crusted cheese from oozing once a wedge has been removed, wrap tightly in plastic cling wrap, pressing it closely to the cut surfaces.
2. To restore full flavour to cheese which has been stored in the refrigerator, remove the pack of cheese at least two hours before serving. Allow it to stand until it returns to room temperature, then unwrap and serve.
3. To make sure a cheese sauce does not go either 'oily' or 'ropey', add the grated cheese to the hot *cooked* sauce, remove from the heat, and stir until the cheese has melted. The sauce will soon become smooth again.
4. If cheese becomes hard and unfit for table use, grate it, mix with dry breadcrumbs and keep in a small container to use up quickly on vegetables, grills and gratin dishes.

HINTS ON STEWS

1. Cheaper cuts of meat, which are excellent for stewing, frequently contain a high percentage of fat. When the stew is cooked, allow it to become completely cold; the solidified fat can then easily be removed with a slotted draining spoon.
2. If there is no time to cool a cooked stew, pour it into a deep narrow vessel. The fat will collect and form a deep layer on the surface which can then be removed with a spoon.
3. Fat taken from a stew can be clarified for frying or roasting. Bring it to the boil in fresh water and allow to boil uncovered for 10 minutes, then cool. When the fat is cold, remove it with a slotted draining spoon, scrape all sediment off the underside, and place the fat on absorbent kitchen paper to dry. This prevents it from 'spitting' when used for frying or roasting.
4. The quickest way of all to remove excess fat from a stew is to drop a few ice cubes into it. The fat will almost immediately solidify, clinging to the ice cubes, which can be quickly removed with a slotted draining spoon. Using layers of absorbent kitchen paper to soak up surplus fat is the most wasteful method.

A batch-baking session with biscuits and pastry

Rule 6

Study the art of presentation. Having achieved a good balance nutritionally, do bear in mind 'appetite appeal'. It has been proved that food which looks unattractive actually discourages healthy appetites by failing to stimulate the digestive juices, making food literally hard to swallow. Food should look as good as it tastes. The simplest meal will be appreciated if attractively served and good presentation helps enormously to disguise the fact that your meal has been prepared with a budget in mind.

At the planning stage you will have decided on interesting contrasts of flavour – savoury, sweet or sour; and contrasting textures – chewy, crisp, hard or soft. Colour is also important. For instance it would be visually unexciting to sit down to green pea soup, followed by green salad and gooseberry fool. Savoury dishes that lack colour can be cheered up by an appropriate garnish, such as parsley, tomato or lemon wedges, tiny croûtons of fried bread, hard-boiled egg, watercress, cucumber or grated cheese. Puddings are easy to decorate with silver balls or tiny jelly sweets, whipped cream, nuts, cocoa or grated chocolate.

A thoughtfully laid table can also increase the enjoyment of a meal. Now that most people lead such busy and varied lives, mealtimes are often the only moments when the whole family sits down together, so try to make them relaxing, social occasions. Matching table cloths, mats and napkins set off the plainest china, and with today's non-iron fabrics and paper napkins, this is no problem. A dish of polished apples or mixed fruit, or a shallow bowl of garden or wild flowers makes a pretty centrepiece to the table, and a couple of candles add a touch of glamour at a special evening meal.

Food should be fun, both to prepare and to eat, so be adventurous and continually experiment with new dishes, or serve up old favourites in new ways.

How to cook better on a budget

Essential basic equipment

It is a waste of time, temper and money to use inefficient cooking aids. You may not be able to invest in all the large pieces of equipment you want at the same time, unless you move house and have to plan a kitchen 'from scratch'. But investigate thoroughly the practical points in favour of any cooker, refrigerator or freezer before you decide to buy.

A cooker with self-cleaning oven linings saves the unpleasant weekly task of cleaning out the oven. If you cannot afford this type of cooker, cook in covered dishes, casseroles or even a dimpled roaster as often as possible. A sheet of foil in the bottom of the oven lasts a long time and saves cleaning burnt-on food spills. If you find bending difficult, a split-level oven and hob unit may save you back trouble and thus justify the extra initial investment. Look carefully at gas hobs, as automatic ignition and easy removal of parts for cleaning save work, and the not inconsiderable cost of cleaning materials. Modern electric hobs can have high-speed rings which make a saving in fuel spent heating up, especially if you learn to judge the best way to use up residual heat as they cool down. Rings of different sizes are desirable because you need only heat the area exactly to fit the bottom of the pan you are using. The same care should be exercised when using an electric oven because much heat is wasted if you only begin cooking when the oven has come up to the correct temperature and only switch off when your food is cooked. There is considerable heat to be made use of while the oven cools down.

Although a big refrigerator may be necessary if you have no freezer, you will often find that buying a freezer cuts down your requirement on refrigerator space. A chest freezer provides cheaper storage than an upright considered in terms of cubic feet/litres because it is cheaper to manufacture. The layout of your kitchen and the availability of space within reasonable distance of it for a large chest freezer must govern your choice of chest or upright, rather than the initial cost of the freezer itself. Small freezers, like refrigerators, are now available and can be placed beneath a working surface. These appliances could be positioned side-by-side if there is no wall space to accommodate the convenient freezer/fridge.

All foods keep very much better when covered, so gradually acquire a selection of suitably shaped containers which make good use of your refrigerator storage space as well as being essential in your freezer.

Smaller equipment to save time and money

There are a number of smaller pieces of equipment that definitely save fuel, now an important economic consideration. The electric slow-cooking pot cooks a family-sized main dish over a number of hours for no more electricity than you would use by leaving one light switched on. For the housewife who has to be out all day working, or is occasionally out all day for other reasons, it is a positive boon.

The pressure cooker which became less fashionable with the availability of frozen vegetables, is back in favour because it uses less fuel than cooking in several saucepans (once you have mastered the knack of using the trivet and separate baskets).

A steamer which cooks more than one item at the same time requires only enough heat to keep a small quantity of water simmering gently. Some economical housewives seem to be able to build up a steam stack reaching almost to the ceiling!

It may seem hardly worth troubling with this particular economy, but using an electric toaster is really a great saving compared to using the grill just for toast.

Perhaps the greatest modern cooking aid is the electric food mixer – the equivalent of another pair of hands in the kitchen. Whichever type you choose, to get the most out of it you must use it regularly, and that means siting it conveniently in the kitchen near a power point. Small mixers are often available with a wall-hanging fitment, so they are always to hand. Some ranges of kitchen units have special fitments to house the largest mixers. These swing out, obviating the need for any lifting.

The simplest mixer is of course the hand-held type, which is used primarily for whisking although it will handle creaming and rubbing-in too. It can be used with any type of mixing bowl or saucepan, either on the worktop or the cooker. As it must be held all the time when in operation, take care to choose one that is not too heavy or cumbersome. Some models stand on end between mixings and need not be tipped awkwardly into a basin. Other models are available with a stand and bowl attachment, but this does not mean that a hand mixer suddenly becomes a table model – it is still limited to lighter duties.

A large table mixer is the best choice if you have a lot of cooking to do, as it copes with practically anything, even to mixing large quantities of dough for bread making. It also comes with a comprehensive list of attachments, which make light work of food preparation: juice extractor (to remove juice from citrus fruits); juice separator (to extract juices from apples, carrots, etc.); coffee grinder; mincer; shredder; potato peeler; can opener and, of course, the blender/liquidizer.

This last attachment, which, like many of the others, is also available as a separate unit, is incredibly versatile. Use it for making soups, drinks, purées and baby foods, for

A selection of useful kitchen equipment

Some basic cooking tools and utensils

cutting up fruit and vegetables, for chopping nuts and for making breadcrumbs and sauces. With a liquidizer it is much easier to save money by preparing at home food which you would otherwise have bought ready-made. The largest and most powerful liquidizer you can afford is the best buy, even if you can then only afford a hand mixer.

Kitchen tools and utensils

A good selection of tools and utensils make cooking easier because it is often time-wasting or impossible to manage without some essential implement. Do not be misled into buying cheap utensils which will wear out quickly and have to be replaced. It is much more economical to buy sturdy well-made articles which will last well.

Here is my check list:
Set of 4 saucepans and steamer
Omelette pan, shallow frying pan, deep-frying pan with
    cover
Ovenproof casseroles (also flameproof if possible)
Mixing bowls, pudding basins (preferably plastic boiling
    basins)
Roasting tin, cake tins and baking trays (preferaby non-
    stick)
Wire cooling trays
Knives, to include several sizes and some serrated
Potato peeler, grater, lemon squeezer
Knife sharpener/bottle opener, can opener
Chopping boards
Wooden kitchen tools (spoons, mallet)
Slotted draining spoon, fish slice, palette knife, ladle
Colander, sieve, strainer
Kitchen scales, measuring jugs, spoons
Kitchen scissors, skewers
Balloon egg whisk and rotary beater
Rolling pin, pastry cutters (or use suitably-sized glasses and
    cups)

HINTS ON VEGETABLES
1. To clean new potatoes without losing the nutritional value just below the delicate skin, rub gently with a nylon scouring pad, and rinse before cooking.
2. To bake small potatoes which might otherwise fall between the bars of an oven grid, arrange them in the cups of a bun tin. This is a useful hint when the oven will only be in use for a short time, insufficient to cook larger potatoes.
3. To ripen green tomatoes, wrap each one separately in tissue paper or absorbent kitchen paper. Place them together in the bottom of a drawer (with newspaper over the top) in a warm room. Examine the tomatoes at intervals and use those which have become ripe.
4. When your stock of root vegetables is reduced to a couple of carrots, one onion and part of a swede or turnip, make a macédoine of mixed diced vegetables, and cook them together with the colourful addition of some frozen peas.

Cook-ahead meals with an auto-timer

Auto-timed meals are a great aid to the budget-minded woman who goes out to work. Nothing is more likely to encourage you to make do with expensive cuts of meat and canned foods than arriving home late with only half an hour in hand to prepare the family's evening meal. Once you have plans for a few basic meals which can all be prepared together in an oven which switches itself on at the time you decide, you can benefit by spending as little as fifteen minutes packing the oven before you leave home. The important factor from the point of view of fuel economy is to *pack* the oven, taking advantage of warmer and cooler sections if yours does not have one of the new features which circulate and distribute heat evenly.

The only drawbacks are as follows:

The food must not spoil if it has to stand for hours on end in a cold oven before heating starts. It must not be food which requires to be put into a hot preheated oven. Lastly, it is very important that all the food is planned to cook in the same length of time. This occasionally means preparing food to a certain point before putting it into the oven, or making sure that it goes into the cooler part so that it will not be over-cooked.

Here are some ideas for items that are so adaptable they can always be fitted into the menu:

1. Soups – prepared vegetables in stock can hardly be over-cooked and the temperature range is not crucial. You always have the choice of serving the soup as it comes from the oven or liquidizing it to make a smooth creamy mixture.
2. For cold-start main dishes a roast is ideal. A joint of pork with crackling, brushed with oil and sprinkled with salt, is excellent. A chicken with a few strips of streaky bacon over the top and a cap of foil is another good choice, but any joint of meat will cook successfully by this method.
3. Most covered casserole dishes are often cooked in the oven anyway. If you wish to keep cubed meat juicy rather than enrich the gravy, toss the meat lightly in fat or oil until sealed before putting it in the dish.
4. Baked potatoes can be used to fit in with any auto-timed plan because you can vary the size of the potato according to the oven heat and length of cooking time.
5. Of fresh vegetables, braised red cabbage or celery most enjoy long slow cooking.
6. Milk puddings made with cereals do not object to cooking a little longer than you would otherwise allow. If they become too dry, stir in a little single cream, top-of-the-milk or evaporated milk when serving.
7. Dried fruit and cooking pears are not easily harmed by long slow cooking. It is unnecessary to soak the fruit if it is going to stand in the oven all day in liquid before cooking begins. Leftover cold tea is better for soaking prunes than water. Extra sweetening can be added at serving time in the form of golden syrup. Pears tend to discolour so should always be left covered in a tinted liquid. Try syrup with the addition of a few drops of red food colouring or a little red wine.

The combination of Oaty vegetable soup (page 29), Stuffed breast of lamb (page 40) and Apple charlotte (page 99) is just one example of recipes in this book which continued

continued

HINTS ON SALADS

1. Lettuce is delicate and once it goes limp cannot be revived. Break off leaves, do not cut them – cut stems turn brown within a few hours. Submerge gently in a colander in cold water, lift up and down several times to wash and leave to drain naturally. Washing lettuce under a running tap bruises it.

2. Outer leaves from lettuces, especially the hothouse variety, may not look crisp enough to use in a salad, but should not be discarded. Wash them carefully, shake dry and shred finely with kitchen scissors and use as a base for savoury starters and cold meat dishes.

3. Salad bowls, if made of wood, should rarely or never be washed. Wipe out with a clean piece of absorbent kitchen paper sprinkled with vegetable oil. When not in use, leave a sheet of the paper inside to prevent dust settling on the surface. The outside should also be oiled occasionally.

4. Celery stalks often taste better in salads and soups if the 'strings' are removed. Grasp these at the top of the stem and pull sharply downwards, then reverse the process from bottom to top. You will find you can remove an average of ten tough threads from each stalk.

HINTS ON SAUCES

1. To make dressings or marinades which require to be emulsified (such as French dressing), put the dry ingredients in a screw-top jar, add the lemon juice, vinegar or wine, then the oil. Allow a small headspace for shaking, screw the top down firmly and shake vigorously until the mixture is well blended and thick.

2. To make a smooth or savoury white sauce, put all the ingredients in the pan together, place over a moderate heat and whisk continuously until the sauce comes to the boil and thickens.

3. To prevent a sauce from forming a skin while it is being kept hot, lay a damp circle of greaseproof paper over the entire surface of the sauce. Remove the paper and stir lightly just before using. For sweet sauces, sift a little icing sugar over the surface instead. For savoury white sauces, pour a thin layer of milk over the top. Stir these in just before serving.

4. To thicken hot soups and creamy sauces at the last moment, remove a little of the hot soup from the saucepan and whisk one or two egg yolks into it according to the quantity to be thickened. Return to the saucepan, whisking constantly and remove from the heat before boiling point is reached.

can be adapted to cook together in an auto-timed oven. Cook the soup in the oven instead of on top, adding a little extra milk at the end if necessary, and make the charlotte with raw apples – they will cook in the extra time in the oven.

Home-made soups and sauces

Soup is the most adaptable of dishes. A small quantity makes an appetizing start to the meal. A large bowl of soup is almost a meal in itself, and can easily become the main course, if accompanied by fresh crusty bread and a salad. In fact, with a wedge of cheese to cut into, it provides a satisfying and nutritionally sound meal to please all tastes.

The garnishes for soup are important. They range from a scattering of chopped fresh herbs, or a dusting of paprika pepper (to add a lively touch of contrast in colour and flavour), to fried bread croûtons which make good use of dripping or bacon fat. In many countries, a soup becomes more substantial because the bread left from breakfast is spread with butter and grated cheese, and baked or grilled to make tasty bread croûtes. Dumplings, usually smaller than those served with stews, can also make a complete meal of soup.

Accustomed as we are to the canned and packaged varieties, we tend to forget the many original recipes for hearty country soups which sent out their enticing odours from the old kitchen range of the past. They are so easy to make, and the proportions of the ingredients are not all-important. If too thick, or too highly seasoned, the fault can soon be put right by adding extra water or milk. If too thin to suit your family's taste, the soup can be thickened just before serving by sprinkling in semolina, adding moistened cornflour, or *beurre manié* – small quantities of butter and flour blended to make a thick paste. Just simmer that much longer to make sure the thickening agent is fully cooked.

Canned soups, however, are a boon when time is precious; meat or chicken can be converted into a tasty casserole dish by simply cooking them gently in a favourite canned soup.

Just a word about sauces: vigorous whisking makes them smooth, velvety in texture and just right for pouring. A thicker coating sauce needs a little less liquid. And if they have to be kept waiting, a circle of dampened greaseproof paper laid over the surface in the saucepan keeps them from forming a skin.

Tomato vichyssoise; Cold cucumber and prawn soup

Cold cucumber and prawn soup

Cold soups are becoming extremely popular and give the enterprising cook an opportunity to introduce delicate flavours and colours to the menu.

Metric	Imperial
1 large cucumber, peeled and halved	*1 large cucumber, peeled and halved*
6 spring onions, trimmed	*6 spring onions, trimmed*
900 ml chicken stock	*1½ pints chicken stock*
1 × 5 ml spoon dried dill	*1 teaspoon dried dill*
25 g cornflour	*1 oz cornflour*
3 × 15 ml spoons water	*3 tablespoons water*
Salt and freshly ground black pepper	*Salt and freshly ground black pepper*
Few drops of green food colouring	*Few drops of green food colouring*
50 g peeled prawns	*2 oz peeled prawns*
4 × 15 ml spoons single cream to garnish	*4 tablespoons single cream to garnish*

Deseed the cucumber and slice. Chop the spring onions, including as much of the green parts as possible, and simmer in the stock with the cucumber and dill until quite tender. Liquidize in an electric blender or pass through a sieve.

Reheat the soup. Moisten the cornflour with the water, add to the soup, stir until boiling and simmer gently for 3 minutes. Remove from the heat and add the seasoning to taste. When cool stir in a few drops of food colouring, and the prawns.

Chill well before serving with a spoonful of cream, swirled into each portion.

Tomato vichyssoise

This fresh-tasting cold soup is not as rich as the classic recipe with cream, but has a delightful pale orange colour and tangy flavour.

Metric	Imperial
50 g butter	*2 oz butter*
3 medium-sized leeks, white part only, washed and sliced	*3 medium-sized leeks, white part only, washed and sliced*
1 medium-sized onion, peeled and finely sliced	*1 medium-sized onion, peeled and finely sliced*
3 medium-sized potatoes, peeled and finely sliced	*3 medium-sized potatoes, peeled and finely sliced*
300 ml chicken stock	*½ pint chicken stock*
Salt and freshly ground white pepper	*Salt and freshly ground white pepper*
Pinch of ground mace	*Pinch of ground mace*
1 bay leaf	*1 bay leaf*
450 ml tomato juice	*¾ pint tomato juice*
300 ml unsweetened natural yogurt	*½ pint unsweetened natural yogurt*
1 × 15 ml spoon snipped chives to garnish	*1 tablespoon snipped chives to garnish*

Heat the butter in saucepan. Add the leeks and the finely sliced onion and potato. Shake the pan over low heat until the vegetables are well coated with the butter. Cover the pan and cook over low heat until tender. Be careful the vegetables do not brown.

Add the stock, seasoning to taste, mace and bay leaf. Cover and simmer for about 20 minutes. Remove the bay leaf. Liquidize the soup in an electric blender or pass through a sieve, then pour into a bowl.

Add the tomato juice and yogurt. Taste and adjust the seasoning if necessary. Chill thoroughly and serve sprinkled with snipped chives.

As an accompaniment, serve brown bread and butter or melba toast.

Chilled beetroot soup

Carrot and orange soup

Chilled beetroot soup

Beetroot has many uses other than in salads, which have so far often been neglected in this country. Now that white and golden varieties are being grown, as well as the familiar ruby red beetroot, this recipe is capable of several delicious variations.

Metric	Imperial
½ kg raw beetroot, peeled	1 lb raw beetroot, peeled
900 ml water	1½ pints water
1 beef stock cube, crumbled	1 beef stock cube, crumbled
1 × 2.5 ml spoon sugar	½ teaspoon sugar
1 medium-sized onion, peeled and chopped	1 medium-sized onion, peeled and chopped
1 × 2.5 ml spoon dried, or 1 × 5 ml spoon fresh dill	½ teaspoon dried, or 1 teaspoon fresh dill
3 cloves	3 cloves
1 × 15 ml spoon malt vinegar	1 tablespoon malt vinegar
Salt and freshly ground black pepper	Salt and freshly ground black pepper
TO FINISH:	TO FINISH:
1 pickled cucumber, chopped	1 pickled cucumber, chopped
1 hard-boiled egg, shelled and chopped	1 hard-boiled egg, shelled and chopped
150 ml unsweetened natural yogurt	¼ pint unsweetened natural yogurt

Finely grate the raw beetroot. Bring the water to the boil, dissolve the crumbled stock cube and sugar in it. Add the beetroot, chopped onion, dill and cloves, and bring back to the boil. Simmer, covered, for 45 minutes.

Allow the soup to cool slightly and strain through a fine sieve. Add the vinegar and seasoning to taste. Chill in the refrigerator.

Before serving, stir the chopped pickled cucumber and hard-boiled egg into the soup and swirl with the yogurt.

Carrot and orange soup

Although this soup, with its velvety consistency and the blended flavours of young vegetables, is so good cold, it is also very pleasant served hot.

Metric	Imperial
25 g butter	1 oz butter
1 clove of garlic, crushed	1 glove of garlic, crushed
1 medium-sized onion, peeled and chopped	1 medium-sized onion, peeled and chopped
½ kg carrots, peeled and coarsely grated	1 lb carrots, peeled and coarsely grated
900 ml water	1½ pints water
2 × 15 ml spoons orange juice and finely grated zest of 1 orange	2 tablespoons orange juice and finely grated zest of 1 orange
1 × 5 ml spoon tomato purée	1 teaspoon of tomato purée
1 chicken stock cube, crumbled	1 chicken stock cube, crumbled
Salt and freshly ground black pepper	Salt and freshly ground black pepper
1 × 5 ml spoon cornflour	1 teaspoon cornflour
2 × 15 ml spoons cold water	2 tablespoons cold water
150 ml milk	¼ pint milk
1 × 5 ml spoon chopped parsley to garnish (optional)	1 teaspoon chopped parsley to garnish (optional)

Melt the butter in a saucepan, add the crushed garlic, chopped onion and grated carrot. Stir and cook, covered, for 5 minutes over a low heat. Add the water, orange juice and zest, tomato purée and the stock cube. Season to taste. Simmer, covered, for 30 minutes. Moisten the cornflour with the cold water, stir into the soup and simmer for another 5 minutes. Liquidize the soup in an electric blender or pass through a sieve. Stir in the milk and chill in the refrigerator. Before serving taste and adjust the seasoning and, if liked, sprinkle with the chopped parsley.

Leek and potato cream

This warming vegetable soup is full of nourishment, and being pale and creamy in colour looks very tempting with a coral-pink touch of paprika.

Metric	Imperial
25 g butter	1 oz butter
½ kg leeks, washed and sliced	1 lb leeks, washed and sliced
½ kg potatoes, peeled and sliced	1 lb potatoes, peeled and sliced
1 large onion, peeled and chopped	1 large onion, peeled and chopped
600 ml water	1 pint water
Salt and freshly ground black pepper	Salt and freshly ground black pepper
1 × 5 ml spoon grated nutmeg	1 teaspoon grated nutmeg
1 bay leaf	1 bay leaf
300 ml milk	½ pint milk
TO FINISH:	TO FINISH:
1 × 2.5 ml spoon paprika (optional)	½ teaspoon paprika (optional)
Strips of leek, finely chopped	Strips of leek, finely chopped

Heat the butter in a large saucepan. Add the leek, potato and onion and cook gently, covered, for about 5 minutes. Shake the pan occasionally to prevent the vegetables from sticking. Add the water, seasoning, grated nutmeg and bay leaf and bring to the boil. Simmer, covered, for 30 minutes. Remove the bay leaf. Liquidize in an electric blender or pass through a sieve.

Return the soup to the saucepan, add the milk and reheat. Taste and adjust the seasoning. If liked, sprinkle with a little paprika or garnish with strips of leek before serving.

Leek and potato cream

Cauliflower and green pea soup

Cauliflower and green pea soup

The fresh taste of small green peas gives interest as well as a touch of colour to this variation of the classic cream of cauliflower soup. Canned peas could be used instead of frozen ones.

Metric	Imperial
1 small cauliflower, trimmed and leaves removed	1 small cauliflower, trimmed and leaves removed
600 ml water	1 pint water
1 medium-sized onion, peeled and grated	1 medium-sized onion, peeled and grated
Salt and freshly ground white pepper	Salt and freshly ground white pepper
1 × 5 ml spoon grated nutmeg	1 teaspoon grated nutmeg
50 g butter	2 oz butter
2 × 15 ml spoons flour	2 tablespoons flour
600 ml milk	1 pint milk
100 g frozen green peas	¼ lb frozen green peas
1 egg yolk	1 egg yolk

Break the cauliflower into florets. Put them into a saucepan with the water, grated onion and seasonings. Bring to the boil and simmer, covered, for about 20 minutes or until the cauliflower is just tender. Remove the cauliflower florets with a slotted draining spoon and mash to make into a purée.

Melt the butter in a clean saucepan, stir in the flour and cook for 1 minute. Gradually stir in the water in which the cauliflower florets were cooked, add the milk and bring to the boil, stirring all the time. Reduce the heat, add the cauliflower purée and the frozen green peas and simmer for 10 minutes. Remove from the heat, adjust the seasoning if necessary and stir in the slightly beaten egg yolk. Return to the heat for 1 minute, stirring constantly, but do not allow to boil.

Cheese soup with dumplings

Cheese soup with dumplings

A soup that is almost a meal in itself, which has always been popular in Scotland and deserves to be better known. Children usually love it.

Metric	Imperial
50 g butter	2 oz butter
1 medium-sized onion, peeled and finely chopped	1 medium-sized onion, peeled and finely chopped
25 g flour	1 oz flour
1 × 2.5 ml spoon dry mustard	½ teaspoon dry mustard
900 ml chicken stock	1½ pints chicken stock
300 ml milk	½ pint milk
1 × 2.5 ml spoon salt	½ teaspoon salt
1 × 1.25 ml spoon freshly ground white pepper	¼ teaspoon freshly ground white pepper
1 × 1.25 ml spoon grated nutmeg	¼ teaspoon grated nutmeg
75 g Cheddar cheese, grated	3 oz Cheddar cheese, grated
FOR THE DUMPLINGS:	FOR THE DUMPLINGS:
50 g quick cook oats	2 oz quick cook oats
25 g shredded beef suet	1 oz shredded beef suet
1 × 15 ml spoon grated onion	1 tablespoon grated onion
1 × 15 ml spoon chopped parsley	1 tablespoon chopped parsley
Salt and freshly ground white pepper	Salt and freshly ground white pepper
1 egg	1 egg

Melt the butter in a fairly large saucepan. Add the onion and fry gently until soft but not brown. Stir in the flour and the dry mustard and cook for 1 minute. Gradually add the stock and milk and bring to the boil, stirring constantly. Add the salt, pepper and grated nutmeg, stir well, cover and simmer for 10 minutes.

Meanwhile, make the dumplings. Place the oats, suet, grated onion and chopped parsley in a bowl and season to taste. Beat the egg until fluffy and use to bind the dry ingredients. Divide the mixture into 16 pieces and roll each one into a ball. Drop the balls into boiling salted water and cook gently for 10 to 15 minutes. Remove with a slotted draining spoon and keep warm.

Liquidize the soup in an electric blender, or pass through a sieve and return to the rinsed-out saucepan. Stir in the cheese and reheat without boiling. Taste and adjust the seasoning, and serve topped with the brown dumplings.

Herbed cream of chestnuts

When chestnuts are in season they are sometimes very abundant. Here is an interesting savoury chestnut soup.

Metric	Imperial
40 g butter	1½ oz butter
1 large onion, peeled and sliced	1 large onion, peeled and sliced
2 small carrots, peeled and sliced	2 small carrots, peeled and sliced
1 stalk celery, scrubbed and chopped	1 stalk celery, scrubbed and chopped
½ kg fresh peeled chestnuts	1 lb fresh peeled chestnuts
1 litre beef stock	1¾ pints beef stock
3–4 sprigs of parsley	3–4 sprigs of parsley
Pinch of dried thyme	Pinch of dried thyme
1 bay leaf	1 bay leaf
Salt and freshly ground black pepper	Salt and freshly ground black pepper
Pinch of grated nutmeg	Pinch of grated nutmeg
300 ml single cream or milk	½ pint single cream or milk
TO FINISH:	TO FINISH:
1 large cooking apple	1 large cooking apple
25 g butter	1 oz butter
1 × 5 ml spoon sugar	1 teaspoon sugar
1 × 15 ml spoon chopped parsley	1 tablespoon chopped parsley

Heat the butter in a saucepan. Add the sliced onion and carrot and the chopped celery. Cover and cook for 3 to 4 minutes, shaking the pan occasionally. Add the chestnuts, cook for a further 3 minutes then add the stock, herbs and seasonings and simmer for 20 to 30 minutes, or until the chestnuts are tender. Remove the bay leaf and liquidize the soup in an electric blender or pass through a sieve. Return to the pan, reheat and adjust the seasoning if necessary. Add the cream or milk just before serving. If using cream, do not allow the soup to boil.

Peel, core and slice the apple into rings. Fry in the butter until golden-brown on both sides, sprinkling each side with a little sugar. Float one or two apple slices in each plate of soup and sprinkle with chopped parsley.

Herbed cream of chestnuts

Oaty vegetable soup (below)

Oaty vegetable soup

This traditional, creamy Scottish soup uses oatmeal for thickening, and makes a satisfying meal in a bowl.

Metric	Imperial
15 g butter	*½ oz butter*
1 medium-sized onion, peeled and chopped	*1 medium-sized onion, peeled and chopped*
1 medium-sized carrot, peeled and chopped	*1 medium-sized carrot, peeled and chopped*
1 small turnip, peeled and chopped	*1 small turnip, peeled and chopped*
1 leek, white and pale green part, washed and chopped	*1 leek, white and pale green part, washed and chopped*
25 g medium oatmeal	*1 oz medium oatmeal*
600 ml stock	*1 pint stock*
Salt and freshly ground black pepper	*Salt and freshly ground black pepper*
1 × 5 ml spoon chopped parsley	*1 teaspoon chopped parsley*
450 ml milk	*¾ pint milk*

Melt the butter in a saucepan. Add the prepared vegetables and stir over gentle heat until all the butter is absorbed. Cover the pan and 'sweat' the vegetables for 2 to 3 minutes. Add the oatmeal and stir over moderate heat for a further 3 to 4 minutes. Pour on the stock, stir well and bring to the boil. Reduce the heat and simmer, covered, for 45 minutes. Season to taste and add the parsley.

Heat the milk in another saucepan until almost boiling. Stir into the soup and adjust the seasoning if necessary. Serve piping hot.

Split pea soup with frankfurters

Split pea soup with frankfurters

A very substantial soup, so thick that a spoon will almost stand up in it. A meal in itself.

Metric	Imperial
¼ kg salt belly of pork, cubed	½ lb salt belly of pork, cubed
½ kg green split peas, soaked overnight in cold water to cover	1 lb green split peas, soaked overnight in cold water to cover
4 medium-sized carrots, peeled and chopped	4 medium-sized carrots, peeled and chopped
4 medium-sized onions, peeled and chopped	4 medium-sized onions, peeled and chopped
2 medium-sized leeks, white and pale green part, washed and chopped	2 medium-sized leeks, white and pale green part, washed and chopped
4 stalks celery, scrubbed and chopped	4 stalks celery, scrubbed and chopped
1 small cooking apple, peeled, cored and chopped	1 small cooking apple, peeled, cored and chopped
1 × 15 ml spoon soft brown sugar or treacle	1 tablespoon soft brown sugar or treacle
Sprig of mint	Sprig of mint
Sprig of parsley	Sprig of parsley
Salt and freshly ground black pepper	Salt and freshly ground black pepper
TO FINISH:	TO FINISH:
25 g butter	1 oz butter
2 or 3 frankfurters, cut into 1 cm lengths	2 or 3 frankfurters, cut into ½ inch lengths

Put the cubes of pork into a large saucepan. Cover them with water and bring slowly to the boil. Drain off the water and cover the meat with 2½ litres/4½ pints of fresh cold water.

Rinse the soaked peas under cold running water. Add the peas, vegetables, apple, sugar or treacle, herbs and seasoning to the saucepan and bring to the boil. Remove any scum with a slotted draining spoon. Reduce the heat, cover and simmer gently, stirring occasionally, for about 2 hours or until the peas are soft and pulpy. The time will depend upon the quality and freshness of the dried peas.

Taste and adjust the seasoning. Remove the herbs and stir in the butter and frankfurters. Reheat and serve very hot with wholemeal bread.
Serves 8

Savoury white sauce

This easy version of the classic Béchamel is very simple to make but has the authentic flavour.

Metric	Imperial
600 ml milk	1 pint milk
1 small onion, peeled and chopped	1 small onion, peeled and chopped
2 cloves	2 cloves
1 bay leaf	1 bay leaf
3 peppercorns	3 peppercorns
25 g butter	1 oz butter
20 g flour	¾ oz flour
Salt and freshly ground black pepper	Salt and freshly ground black pepper

Place the milk, onion, cloves, bay leaf and peppercorns in a saucepan. Bring to the boil and remove from the heat. Cover the pan and allow to stand until cool.

Strain the flavoured milk into a clean saucepan and add the butter and flour. Place over moderate heat and whisk constantly until the sauce comes to the boil. Cook gently for 2 minutes until smooth and thickened, stirring occasionally. Season to taste. .

Makes 600 ml/1 pint

NOTE: If the sauce is required quickly, simply add a crumbled chicken stock cube to the cold milk, add the butter and flour and continue as above. This reduces the number of ingredients to four and the sauce can be made in 5 minutes.

Cheese sauce
Stir 1 × 5 ml spoon/1 teaspoon made mustard and 100 g/¼ lb grated cheese into the basic sauce. If liked, add 1 × 2.5 ml spoon/½ teaspoon grated nutmeg.

Mushroom sauce
Sprinkle 175 g/6 oz sliced button mushrooms with 1 × 15 ml spoon/1 tablespoon lemon juice and sauté in 50 g/2 oz butter until golden and stir into the basic sauce. If liked, add 1 × 15 ml spoon/1 tablespoon dry sherry.

Onion sauce
Boil 1 large, peeled and chopped onion in just sufficient water to cover until tender. Drain well and stir into the basic sauce. If liked, add 2 × 15 ml spoons/2 tablespoons single cream or evaporated milk.

Egg sauce
Stir 2 shelled and chopped hard-boiled eggs into the basic sauce. If liked, add 2 × 15 ml spoons/2 tablespoons chopped parsley.

Savoury white sauce

Rich lemon sauce

Here is a more unusual sauce which is a perfect accompaniment for fried or grilled fish, or any chicken dish. Substitute orange for lemon if you prefer a sweeter rich sauce to serve with duck or pork.

Metric	Imperial
300 ml water	½ pint water
1 chicken stock cube, crumbled	1 chicken stock cube, crumbled
Thinly pared rind of ½ lemon	Thinly pared rind of ½ lemon
25 g butter	1 oz butter
20 g flour	¾ oz flour
3 × 15 ml spoons lemon juice	3 tablespoons lemon juice
1 egg yolk	1 egg yolk
2 × 15 ml spoons single cream or evaporated milk	2 tablespoons single cream or evaporated milk
Salt and freshly ground white pepper	Salt and freshly ground white pepper

Place the water, crumbled stock cube, lemon rind, butter and flour into a saucepan. Place over a moderate heat and whisk constantly until the sauce comes to the boil. Cook gently for 2 minutes until thickened and smooth, stirring frequently.

Beat together the lemon juice and egg yolk in a bowl, beat in a little of the hot sauce then return this mixture to the pan and reheat without boiling. Stir in the cream or evaporated milk and season to taste.

Makes 450 ml / ¾ pint

Rich lemon sauce

Simple sweet white sauce; Chocolate sauce; Coffee sauce

Simple sweet white sauce

A basic sauce which goes well with hot puddings and sweet pastry dishes and is quick to make. It is easily adapted to various flavours.

Metric	Imperial
600 ml milk	1 pint milk
2 × 15 ml spoons caster sugar	2 tablespoons caster sugar
25 g cornflour	1 oz cornflour

Place the milk, sugar and cornflour in a saucepan. Whisk over moderate heat until the sauce comes to the boil. Simmer for 2 minutes until smooth and thickened, stirring all the time. To make a basic vanilla sauce, add 1 × 2.5 ml spoon / ½ teaspoon vanilla essence and stir well.

Sherried custard sauce

This sauce can accompany delicate sponge puddings or rich Christmas pudding equally well. The flavour can be varied by adding Marsala or Madeira instead of sherry.

Metric	Imperial
300 ml milk	½ pint milk
2 egg yolks, beaten	2 egg yolks, beaten
2 × 15 ml spoons caster sugar	2 tablespoons caster sugar
2 × 15 ml spoons sweet sherry	2 tablespoons sweet sherry

Place the milk in a saucepan and bring just to boiling point. Beat together the egg yolks and sugar, then add a little of the scalded milk and beat well. Add this mixture to the rest of the milk and cook over a pan of simmering water until the sauce will coat the back of a wooden spoon, stirring all the time. Do not boil. Remove from the heat, cover the surface with a circle of greaseproof paper and allow to cool.

When the sauce is cold, stir in the sherry.

Sherried custard sauce

Coffee sauce
Dissolve 2 × 5 ml spoons / 2 teaspoons instant coffee powder in 1 × 15 ml spoon / tablespoon boiling water and stir into the basic sauce with 15 g / ½ oz unsalted butter. Stir until smooth.

Chocolate sauce
Add 1 × 15 ml spoon / 1 tablespoon cocoa with the cornflour when making up the basic sauce. To make a nutty-flavoured chocolate sauce add half an 85 g / 3 oz bar of hazelnut or peanut chocolate, broken into squares. Stir into the hot sauce until melted.

Hearty main dishes

It has been said that 'the casserole is the pauper's pot of gold'. It is certainly worth its weight in gold, when it comes to providing tasty, filling main dishes at little cost. Some of the stews and casseroles your family will enjoy most are planned to cook on the hob, others in the oven because oven heat should never be wasted. It all depends whether you have other casseroles, jacket potatoes, or a baked pudding to cook at the same time. Many of these dishes could be cooked either way. But it is a useful tip to remember that stews cooked on top of the stove may tend to stick and burn if fully thickened at the start. You may prefer to leave part of the thickening until the end of cooking, but such recipes are easy to adapt. (This difficulty does not occur in oven cooking, of course, where the source of heat is not directly under the casserole dish.)

Meat goes a long way when combined with vegetables, and the flavour is improved when the juices are allowed to mingle in long, slow cooking. Most of the stews for which recipes are given in this book could be cooked in an electric slow cooker, bearing in mind that the preliminary browning and bringing to the boil of liquid before the ingredients are transferred to the slow cooker, give it the necessary good start. After that, it can cook on undisturbed for many hours, at very little fuel cost, and this is extremely useful if part of the food has to be kept hot without drying out for latecomers.

Besides adding vegetables, there are various ways to make meat, or other expensive basic ingredients go further. All sorts of pastry crusts, including suet and potato pastry, and dumplings for instance. A scone mix provides a cobbler top, and it is a great economy to make up a larger quantity of the dough and bake some tea-time scones as well. They keep fresh and moist if stored in polythene bags.

Piped mashed potato toppings are not only an integral part of the main course, but extremely decorative features. Allow time for the mashed potato to cool slightly, or you will burn your fingers when piping it. For this reason the pie usually goes back in the oven or under the grill to reheat and turn golden-brown. Potato slices can be arranged overlapping to make decorative patterns too. And even if the recipe does not demand it, pastry brushed over with egg wash (equal amount of egg yolk and cold water combined) or with cold milk, takes a better colour in the oven.

Do not neglect the recipes using offal, an awful word, quite rightly rejected by American housewives in favour of the description 'variety meats'. These meats really are extremely nourishing, relatively cheap, and quite delicious when well cooked.

Chicken hot-pot

This recipe produces a dish which feeds four amply and leaves sufficient for at least two more portions to be reheated and served later. The carcase and giblets of the fowl can be used to make soup.

Metric	Imperial
2–2½ kg boiling fowl	4–5 lb boiling fowl
25 g butter	1 oz butter
Salt and freshly ground black pepper	Salt and freshly ground black pepper
3 large onions, peeled and thickly sliced	3 large onions, peeled and thickly sliced
¾ kg potatoes, peeled and thickly sliced	1½ lb potatoes, peeled and thickly sliced
1 × 5 ml spoon ground bay leaves	1 teaspoon ground bay leaves
Grated zest and juice of 1 lemon	Grated zest and juice of 1 lemon
1 chicken stock cube	1 chicken stock cube
450 ml boiling water	¾ pint boiling water
1 × 15 ml spoon chopped parsley to garnish	1 tablespoon chopped parsley to garnish

Joint the boiling fowl into 8 pieces; 2 breasts, 2 wings, 2 thighs and 2 drumsticks.

Grease a deep casserole with a little of the butter and place half the joints in the bottom. Season lightly and cover with a layer of onion slices, then with a layer of potato slices. Sprinkle with half the ground bay leaves and lemon zest. Put the remaining chicken pieces on top, season and again cover with a layer of onion slices then potato slices. Dissolve the stock cube in the hot water, add the lemon juice and pour into the casserole. Sprinkle with the remaining lemon zest and bay leaves and dot with the rest of the butter. Cover the casserole with a sheet of foil and put on the lid.

Bake in a warm oven (160°C/325°F or Gas Mark 3) for 2 hours. Remove the foil cover and lid, and cook for a further 30 minutes to brown the top. (An old boiling fowl may take even longer, so test with a fork to make sure it is tender before cooking the dish uncovered for the last 30 minutes.)

Serve sprinkled with the chopped parsley.

Chicken hot-pot

Spiced chicken pot roast

A small oven-ready chicken can be transformed into a substantial dish with an oriental flavour using this spicy rice stuffing.

Metric	Imperial
1½–1¾ kg roasting chicken with giblets	3–3½ lb roasting chicken with giblets
1 × 5 ml spoon ground coriander	1 teaspoon ground coriander
1 × 5 ml spoon ground cumin seed	1 teaspoon ground cumin seed
50 g butter	2 oz butter
225 g cooked long-grain rice	½ lb cooked long-grain rice
1 small green pepper, deseeded and cut into strips	1 small green pepper, deseeded and cut into strips
1 × approx. 100 g can red pimientos, drained and chopped	1 × approx. 4 oz can red pimientos, drained and chopped
2 large tomatoes, peeled and chopped	2 large tomatoes, peeled and chopped
Salt and freshly ground black pepper	Salt and freshly ground black pepper
1 large onion, peeled and chopped	1 large onion, peeled and chopped
1 × 15 ml spoon powdered turmeric	1 tablespoon powdered turmeric

Wash the chicken well, wash and drain the giblets, and cook the giblets in lightly salted water for about 20 minutes to make stock.

Meanwhile, prick the chicken all over with a fork. Combine the ground coriander and cumin seed and rub into the chicken.

Melt half the butter in a saucepan. Mix in the cooked rice, strips of green pepper, chopped pimiento and chopped tomato and season well. Use the mixture to stuff the chicken.

Heat the remaining butter in a frying pan. Add the chopped onion and turmeric and cook, stirring constantly, until golden-brown. Add the stuffed chicken, turning frequently, until coated with the mixture. Transfer the chicken with the onion and spices, to a casserole which fits it with little space to spare. Make up the strained giblet stock to 300 ml / ½ pint with boiling water and pour into the frying pan. Stir well and pour over the chicken. Cover tightly and put the casserole into a moderate oven (180°C/350°F or Gas Mark 4) for 1½ hours. Serve with a salad and potatoes in their jackets.

Spiced chicken pot roast

Lamb and leek pudding

Lamb and leek pudding

Less expensive than the traditional steak and kidney pudding, this is equally delicious and satisfying. If the filling does not come high enough up the basin, put in a layer of diced raw potato.

Metric
FOR THE PASTRY:
225 g self-raising flour
1 × 5 ml spoon salt
100 g shredded beef suet
150 ml water
FOR THE FILLING:
3 thin leeks, washed and
  sliced in rings
½ kg boned lamb shoulder
  or best end of neck,
  trimmed of fat and cut
  into small cubes
2 × 15 ml spoons seasoned
  flour for coating
1 beef stock cube,
  crumbled
Salt and freshly ground
  black pepper
1 × 5 ml spoon dried thyme

Imperial
FOR THE PASTRY:
½ lb self-raising flour
1 teaspoon salt
¼ lb shredded beef suet
¼ pint water
FOR THE FILLING:
3 thin leeks, washed and
  sliced in rings
1 lb boned lamb shoulder
  or best end of neck,
  trimmed of fat and cut
  into small cubes
2 tablespoons seasoned
  flour for coating
1 beef stock cube,
  crumbled
Salt and freshly ground
  black pepper
1 teaspoon dried thyme

To make the pastry, sift the flour and salt into a bowl. Stir in the shredded suet. Mix in just sufficient of the water to make a smooth dough that leaves the sides of the bowl clean. Turn out on to a lightly floured board and knead for 1 minute.

Form into 2 balls, 1 twice as large as the other. Roll the larger ball into a round big enough to line a 1 litre / 1¾ pint pudding basin. Grease the pudding basin. Ease the pastry into position, making cuts down the sides of the pastry with clean kitchen scissors, if necessary, and sealing these together after brushing the cut edges with water.

Wash the sliced leeks thoroughly in a colander and drain well. Coat the cubed lamb with seasoned flour. Put both into the basin in alternate layers. Mix the crumbled stock cube, seasoning to taste and the dried thyme, with sufficient cold water to come halfway up the contents. Form the reserved pastry into a lid and place on top, sealing the edges of the pastry with cold water.

Cover the pudding with greased foil, making a pleat in the centre to allow for expansion. Tie a piece of string tightly round the bowl under the lip and across the top to form a handle. Place in a steamer or large saucepan of simmering water, making sure the water does not come more than halfway up the sides of the basin. Cover and steam for 3 hours, topping up the water level when necessary.

Remove the basin by the string handle, using the handle of a wooden spoon slipped under the string. Take off the foil and serve in wedges, taking care to spoon out a reasonable proportion of the filling with each serving. Diced carrots and peas make a good accompaniment.

Casseroled lamb with pears

This combination may sound unusual, but the mingled flavours of the fruit and French beans with lamb is quite delicious.

Metric	Imperial
1 kg middle and best end neck of lamb	2 lb middle and best end neck of lamb
2 × 5 ml spoons ground ginger	2 teaspoons ground ginger
6 medium-sized cooking pears, peeled and cored	6 medium-sized cooking pears, peeled and cored
4 medium-sized potatoes, peeled and diced	4 medium-sized potatoes, peeled and diced
4 × 15 ml spoons dry cider	4 tablespoons dry cider
Salt and freshly ground black pepper	Salt and freshly ground black pepper
½ kg frozen whole French beans	1 lb frozen whole French beans
2 × 5 ml spoons snipped chives to garnish (optional)	2 teaspoons snipped chives to garnish (optional)

Trim the excess fat from the lamb. In a non-stick, or slightly greased frying pan brown the pieces in their own fat on both sides, then transfer them to a casserole. Sprinkle with the ground ginger. Quarter the cooking pears and place in a layer over the meat. Arrange the diced potatoes over the pears. Add the dry cider and season well.

Cover and cook in a warm oven (160°C/325°F or Gas Mark 3) for 1¼ hours, adding the French beans for the last 30 minutes of cooking time. Taste and adjust the seasoning. If liked, serve garnished with snipped chives.

Casseroled lamb with pears

Chump chops with haricot beans

Chump chops with haricot beans

These meaty chops require thorough cooking. The meat is really tender and has a sweet flavour when casseroled.

Metric	Imperial
4 large chump chops of lamb	4 large chump chops of lamb
50 g long-grain rice	2 oz long-grain rice
4 medium-sized onions, peeled and cut into quarters	4 medium-sized onions, peeled and cut into quarters
¼ kg haricot beans, soaked overnight and drained	½ lb haricot beans, soaked overnight and drained
1 × 425 g can tomatoes	1 × 15 oz can tomatoes
300 ml beef stock	½ pint beef stock
Salt and freshly ground black pepper	Salt and freshly ground black pepper
Chopped parsley to garnish	Chopped parsley to garnish

Trim the chops of excess fat. Render out the fat in a frying pan, and use to fry the chops for about 5 minutes, turning until brown on both sides. Transfer to a casserole.

Put the rice into the fat remaining in the pan, and stir over moderate heat for 2 to 3 minutes, or until transparent and just beginning to turn golden. Add to the casserole with the onions, haricot beans, tomatoes and their liquid and the stock. Season well. Cover and cook in a moderate oven (180°C/350°F or Gas Mark 4) for 1 to 1½ hours or until the beans are tender. Taste and adjust the seasoning if necessary. Serve sprinkled with chopped parsley.

Barbecued lamb spare ribs

Breast of lamb produces a less expensive version of the popular dish, barbecued spare ribs of pork. The flavour is delicate and the meat tastes particularly succulent cooked in this way.

Metric	Imperial
1 large breast of lamb, cut into ribs	1 large breast of lamb, cut into ribs
600 ml water	1 pint water
1 × 15 ml spoon malt vinegar	1 tablespoon malt vinegar
FOR THE SAUCE:	FOR THE SAUCE:
1 × 15 ml spoon soya sauce	1 tablespoon soya sauce
1 × 15 ml spoon clear honey	1 tablespoon clear honey
1 × 15 ml spoon plum or other red jam	1 tablespoon plum or other red jam
1 × 5 ml spoon malt vinegar	1 teaspoon malt vinegar
1 × 2.5 ml spoon Worcestershire sauce	½ teaspoon Worcestershire sauce
	½ teaspoon dry mustard
	½ teaspoon tomato ketchup
	½ teaspoon lemon juice

1 × 2.5 ml spoon dry mustard
1 × 2.5 ml spoon tomato ketchup
1 × 2.5 ml spoon lemon juice
Salt and freshly ground black pepper

Salt and freshly ground black pepper

Remove any excess skin and fat from the ribs. Put the water and vinegar into a saucepan and bring to the boil. Place the ribs in the boiling water and simmer, covered, for 15 minutes. Remove the ribs and drain well. Place them in a roasting tin.

Mix together all the ingredients for the sauce in a small saucepan and simmer for 4 minutes. Taste and adjust the seasoning if necessary.

Pour the sauce over the meat and cook, covered, in a moderate oven (180°C/350°F or Gas Mark 4) for 30 minutes. Increase the temperature to (200°C/400°F or Gas Mark 6) and cook for a further 20 minutes. Transfer to a hot serving platter, and serve with plain boiled rice.

Barbecued lamb spare ribs

Stuffed breast of lamb

Oven heat for roasting a joint is more economically used if potatoes are baked in their jackets at the same time, and an egg custard, milk pudding, or compote of fruit placed in the cooler part of the oven.

Metric	Imperial
1 kg breast of lamb, boned and trimmed	*2 lb breast of lamb, boned and trimmed*
Salt and freshly ground black pepper	*Salt and freshly ground black pepper*
4 large potatoes, scrubbed	*4 large potatoes, scrubbed*
Parsley sprigs to garnish	*Parsley sprigs to garnish*
FOR THE STUFFING:	FOR THE STUFFING:
100 g fresh white breadcrumbs	*¼ lb fresh white breadcrumbs*
1 small onion, peeled and finely chopped	*1 small onion, peeled and finely chopped*
1 medium-sized carrot, peeled and grated	*1 medium-sized carrot, peeled and grated*
1 medium-sized turnip, peeled and grated	*1 medium-sized turnip, peeled and grated*
1 × 15 ml spoon chopped parsley	*1 tablespoon chopped parsley*
1 × 2.5 ml spoon dried sage	*½ teaspoon dried sage*
Salt and freshly ground black pepper	*Salt and freshly ground black pepper*
1 egg, lightly beaten	*1 egg, lightly beaten*

Sew the breast of lamb together to make one piece, if necessary, and sprinkle with a little seasoning. Prick the potatoes well.

To make the stuffing, mix together the breadcrumbs, chopped onion, grated carrot, grated turnip, chopped parsley and sage. Season with salt and pepper. Bind together with the lightly beaten egg. Spread the stuffing over the inside of the breast of lamb. Roll up tightly and secure with string. Place into a roasting tin. Put the potatoes round the joint. Bake in a moderate oven (180°C/350°F or Gas Mark 4) for 1 hour. Turn the potatoes over to coat evenly with the pan juices. Bake for another 45 minutes. Serve garnished with parsley sprigs.

Stuffed breast of lamb

Pork and apple casserole

Pork and apple casserole

If the juniper berries called for in this recipe are not available, use a few cloves instead, but remember they will add a slightly sweeter flavour to the dish.

Metric	Imperial
25 g dripping or lard	1 oz dripping or lard
4 thick slices belly pork	4 thick slices belly pork
1 clove of garlic, crushed	1 clove of garlic, crushed
4 juniper berries	4 juniper berries
2 medium-sized onions, peeled and chopped	2 medium-sized onions, peeled and chopped
2 medium-sized cooking apples, peeled, cored and chopped	2 medium-sized cooking apples, peeled, cored and chopped
Salt and freshly ground black pepper	Salt and freshly ground black pepper
150 ml apple juice	¼ pint apple juice
1 kg potatoes, peeled and thickly sliced	2 lb potatoes, peeled and thickly sliced
15 g butter	½ oz butter

Melt the dripping or lard in a frying pan. Add the pork slices and fry until golden-brown on both sides.

Arrange the meat in a shallow casserole. Add the crushed garlic and juniper berries and cover with a layer of chopped onion and apple. Season to taste. Pour on the apple juice and cover with overlapping potato slices. Dot with butter, cover and bake in a cool oven (160°C/325°F or Gas Mark 3) for 1½ hours. Remove the lid and cook for a further 30 minutes to brown the top.

Ham and beef fricassée

The stock from a ham bone may be sufficient to provide the basis for a tasty vegetable soup as well as being used for this recipe. Vegetables can be cooked in the saucepan with the bone, which is then removed and the soup liquidized or sieved.

Metric	Imperial
1 ham bone with a little meat	1 ham bone with a little meat
1 bouquet garni	1 bouquet garni
1 small onion, peeled	1 small onion, peeled
1 slice of white bread, crust removed	1 slice of white bread, crust removed
1 × 15 ml spoon corn oil	1 tablespoon corn oil
½ kg lean minced beef	1 lb lean minced beef
2 × 15 ml spoons seedless raisins	2 tablespoons seedless raisins
1 × 15 ml spoon flour	1 tablespoon flour
Salt and freshly ground black pepper	Salt and freshly ground black pepper

On a clean chopping board remove all the lean meat from the ham bone. Put the bone on to boil with enough water just to cover it. Add the bouquet garni and simmer for 30 minutes.

Mince the ham with the onion, then put the bread through the mincer. Heat the corn oil in a flameproof casserole and fry the minced beef gently until brown, turning constantly. Add the ham mixture and the raisins, sprinkle with the flour, and season to taste. Cook, still stirring, for a further 2 minutes. Measure 150 ml/¼ pint of the ham stock and add to the casserole. Cover and simmer for 30 minutes. Add a little more ham stock if the mixture becomes too dry. Taste and adjust the seasoning if necessary. Serve with piped mashed potatoes.

Ham and beef fricassée

Veal stew with piped potato

A simple and economical stew to serve the family.

Metric	Imperial
½ kg pie veal	1 lb pie veal
1 × 15 ml spoon seasoned flour for coating	1 tablespoon seasoned flour for coating
25 g lard	1 oz lard
1 medium-sized onion, peeled and chopped	1 medium-sized onion, peeled and chopped
1 small parsnip, peeled and diced	1 small parsnip, peeled and diced
1 small turnip, peeled and diced	1 small turnip, peeled and diced
1 × 5 ml spoon caraway seed	1 teaspoon caraway seed
300 ml beef stock	½ pint beef stock
Salt and freshly ground black pepper	Salt and freshly ground black pepper
1 × 15 ml spoon chopped parsley to garnish	1 tablespoon chopped parsley to garnish
FOR THE MASHED POTATO:	FOR THE MASHED POTATO:
½ kg potatoes	1 lb potatoes
50 g butter	2 oz butter
2 × 15 ml spoons milk	2 tablespoons milk
Salt and freshly ground black pepper	Salt and freshly ground black pepper

Veal stew with piped potato; Veal and vegetable casserole

Turn the veal in the seasoned flour. Melt the lard in a saucepan and quickly brown the meat in it. Add the chopped onion, diced parsnip and turnip and the caraway seed. Cook for a further 3 minutes, stirring all the time. Add the stock, season to taste and simmer, covered, for 1 hour.

While the stew is cooking, boil the potatoes and mash with the butter and milk until smooth and creamy, adding seasoning to taste. When the stew is ready to serve, pipe the mashed potato around the edge of the dish and sprinkle with chopped parsley.

Veal and vegetable casserole

Veal is often a costly meat, but pie veal which usually consists of the meat from the breast, shoulder and knuckle, has no waste and is not expensive. It makes an interesting change in this cheese-crusted casserole dish.

Metric	Imperial
1 kg pie veal, cubed	*2 lb pie veal, cubed*
Salt and freshly ground black pepper	*Salt and freshly ground black pepper*
2 × 15 ml spoons vegetable oil	*2 tablespoons vegetable oil*
1 clove of garlic, crushed	*1 clove of garlic, crushed*
6 spring onions, trimmed and chopped	*6 spring onions, trimmed and chopped*
2 small turnips, peeled and diced	*2 small turnips, peeled and diced*
¼ kg baby carrots, scrubbed	*½ lb baby carrots, scrubbed*
1 × 2.5 ml spoon dried thyme	*½ teaspoon dried thyme*
1 × 2.5 ml spoon dried marjoram	*½ teaspoon dried marjoram*
4 medium-sized potatoes, peeled and thinly sliced	*4 medium-sized potatoes, peeled and thinly sliced*
300 ml water	*½ pint water*
1 chicken stock cube, crumbled	*1 chicken stock cube, crumbled*
150 ml dry cider	*¼ pint dry cider*
TO FINISH:	TO FINISH:
100 g cottage cheese	*¼ lb cottage cheese*
1 × 5 ml spoon snipped chives	*1 teaspoon snipped chives*
1 × 15 ml spoon chopped parsley	*1 tablespoon chopped parsley*
Salt and freshly ground black pepper	*Salt and freshly ground black pepper*

Sprinkle the meat with salt and pepper. Heat the oil in a large frying pan, add the meat, crushed garlic and chopped spring onions and cook for 5 minutes, turning several times to brown the meat on all sides. Remove with a slotted draining spoon to a casserole.

Cook the diced turnips and carrots in the oil left in the pan for 5 minutes. Add the vegetables to the meat in the casserole, sprinkle in the herbs and cover with a layer of potato slices.

Mix together the water, chicken stock cube and the cider in a saucepan, bring to the boil and pour into the casserole. Cover and cook in a cool oven (150°C/300°F or Gas Mark 2) for 2 hours. Taste and adjust seasoning if necessary.

Mix the cottage cheese with the snipped chives and chopped parsley and a little seasoning, if liked, and spread over the potatoes. Raise the heat to fairly hot (200°C/400°F or Gas Mark 6) for a further 10 minutes to form a cheesy crust. Serve at once.

Bacon collar with apricots

Bacon collar with apricots

Collar of bacon makes a satisfying and economical joint and the strong flavour is well balanced by the mildness of the apricots in this casserole dish.

Metric	Imperial
1–1½ kg joint collar bacon	*2–3 lb joint collar bacon*
1 bouquet garni	*1 bouquet garni*
100 g dried apricots	*¼ lb dried apricots*
½ kg parsnips, peeled and quartered	*1 lb parsnips, peeled and quartered*
25 g sultanas	*1 oz sultanas*
Salt and freshly ground black pepper	*Salt and freshly ground black pepper*
1 × 5 ml spoon cornflour (optional)	*1 teaspoon cornflour (optional)*
1 × 15 ml spoon water (optional)	*1 tablespoon water (optional)*

Soak the joint overnight in cold water. Drain and place in a casserole with the bouquet garni and almost cover with fresh water. Put the lid on the casserole and cook in a moderate oven (180°C/350°F or Gas Mark 4) for 1 hour.

Add the apricots, parsnips, sultanas, a little pepper, and salt if needed. Cook covered, for a further 1 hour. Discard the bouquet garni.

Take out the bacon, remove the rind, slice the meat and place on a heated serving dish garnished with the apricots and parsnips. Serve the sauce separately.

If a slightly thicker sauce is required, moisten the cornflour with the water and stir into the casserole 15 minutes before the joint is done.

Serve with boiled or mashed potatoes, and do not add salt to the water when cooking them in case the bacon sauce is slightly salty.

Fruited beef olives

The extra ingredients in the stuffing for this version of beef olives make the meat go further. The meat should be batted out really thinly to make satisfactory rolls.

Metric	Imperial
350 g topside of beef	¾ lb topside of beef
40 g beef dripping	1½ oz beef dripping
1 medium-sized onion, peeled and roughly chopped	1 medium-sized onion, peeled and roughly chopped
25 g flour	1 oz flour
450 ml beef stock	¾ pint beef stock
2 × 5 ml spoons salt	2 teaspoons salt
Freshly ground black pepper	Freshly ground black pepper
FOR THE STUFFING:	FOR THE STUFFING:
5 × 15 ml spoons fresh white breadcrumbs	5 tablespoons fresh white breadcrumbs
1 × 15 ml spoon shredded beef suet	1 tablespoon shredded beef suet
4 dried apricots, soaked and chopped	4 dried apricots, soaked and chopped
1 rasher lean bacon, diced	1 rasher lean bacon, diced
1 × 5 ml spoon dried or 1 × 15 ml spoon fresh chopped mixed herbs	1 teaspoon dried or 1 tablespoon fresh chopped mixed herbs
Salt and freshly ground black pepper	Salt and freshly ground black pepper
1 egg, lightly beaten	1 egg, lightly beaten
8 stuffed green olives to garnish	8 stuffed green olives to garnish

Cut the meat into slices across the grain, about 7.5 × 10 cm/3 × 4 inches. Flatten the slices by laying them between sheets of greaseproof paper and batting out with a rolling pin.

Prepare the stuffing by mixing all the ingredients together well. Spread over the slices of meat. Roll up the meat tightly and secure the rolls with wooden cocktail sticks or cotton thread.

Melt the dripping in a small casserole and brown the beef olives quickly on all sides. Remove them and fry the chopped onion until limp. Sprinkle in the flour and cook gently for another 2 minutes, stirring constantly, until the flour is golden-brown. Gradually stir in the stock and seasoning to taste. Bring to the boil, add the beef olives, cover with the lid and simmer gently for 2 hours.

Transfer the beef olives to a heated serving dish. Remove the cocktail sticks or cotton thread. Garnish each roll with an olive. Pour over a little of the sauce and serve the remainder separately. If liked, garnish each roll with a parsley sprig instead of an olive.

Minced beef and kidney pie

This mixture is also very good for filling small pies baked in patty tins. It can also be served cold.

Metric	Imperial
225 g flour	½ lb flour
Pinch of salt	Pinch of salt
100 g lard, cut into pieces	¼ lb lard, cut into pieces
2–3 × 15 ml spoons cold water	2–3 tablespoons cold water
FOR THE FILLING:	FOR THE FILLING:
25 g dripping	1 oz dripping
1 small onion, peeled and chopped	1 small onion, peeled and chopped
½ kg minced beef	1 lb minced beef
100 g ox kidney, trimmed and finely chopped	¼ lb ox kidney, trimmed and finely chopped
300 ml water	½ pint water
1 × 5 ml spoon gravy powder	1 teaspoon gravy powder
Salt and freshly ground black pepper	Salt and freshly ground black pepper
1 × 15 ml spoon cornflour	1 tablespoon cornflour
A little milk to glaze	A little milk to glaze
Parsley sprigs to garnish	Parsley sprigs to garnish

Sift the flour and salt into a bowl. Rub in the lard until the mixture resembles fine breadcrumbs. Stir in just sufficient water to hold the mixture together, then form into a smooth ball. Wrap in foil or greaseproof paper and chill in the refrigerator for 30 minutes.

Meanwhile, melt the dripping in a saucepan. Add the chopped onion and fry, stirring constantly, for 3 to 4 minutes. Add the minced beef and kidney and continue to fry, stirring until all the meat is brown and no lumps remain. Add the water, gravy powder and seasoning. Bring to the boil and stir well. Cover and simmer for 1 hour. Alternatively, cook in a pressure cooker for 20 minutes.

Blend the cornflour with a little cold water. Add to the meat mixture and stir constantly until thickened. Simmer for a further 3 minutes. Cool.

Divide the pastry into two and roll out one half on a floured surface to form a circle to fit the base of a 20 cm/8 inch pie dish. Spoon in the meat mixture. Roll out the remaining pastry for the lid. Lay this over the filling, dampen the edges and press well together to seal. Flute the edge with finger and thumb or with a fork. Decorate the top using any pastry trimmings.

Brush the pie with milk and make a slit in the centre for the steam to escape.

Place the pie dish on a baking sheet and bake in a fairly hot oven (200°C/400°F or Gas Mark 6) for 20 minutes, or until golden-brown on top. Serve garnished with sprigs of parsley.

Minced beef and kidney pie; Fruited beef olives

Beefy cottage pie

This pie is just as good made ahead of time, to the point of putting in the oven when it can be slipped into a polythene bag and placed in the refrigerator overnight. It will then require 30 minutes to reheat and brown in a hot oven.

Metric
2 × 15 ml spoons vegetable oil
2 medium-sized onions, peeled and sliced
½ kg lean minced beef
1 × 15 ml spoon tomato purée
1 × 5 ml spoon sugar
1 × 5 ml spoon Worcestershire sauce
Salt and freshly ground black pepper
150 ml hot water
1 × 5 ml spoon Bovril or Marmite
½ kg cooked potatoes, mashed and seasoned
3 × 15 ml spoons hot milk

Imperial
2 tablespoons vegetable oil
2 medium-sized onions, peeled and sliced
1 lb lean minced beef
1 tablespoon tomato purée
1 teaspoon sugar
1 teaspoon Worcestershire sauce
Salt and freshly ground black pepper
¼ pint hot water
1 teaspoon Bovril or Marmite
1 lb cooked potatoes, mashed and seasoned
3 tablespoons hot milk

Heat the oil in a heavy saucepan or flameproof casserole. Add the sliced onions and fry until soft. Add the minced beef and fry gently for 5 minutes, breaking it up with a wooden spoon as it cooks. When all the meat has turned colour, add all the remaining ingredients except the mashed potato and milk. Cover and simmer for 30 minutes or until the meat is tender and most of the liquid absorbed. Taste and adjust the seasoning if necessary. Turn into a pie dish.

Beat the hot milk into the mashed potato, reserving 1 × 15 ml spoons / 1 tablespoon and spread the creamed potato over the meat. Brush with the remaining milk and bake in a hot oven (220°C/425°F or Gas Mark 7) for 10 minutes.

Beef with cheese cobbler

A really satisfying dish, containing meat and cheese in such a way that only a green vegetable, such as Brussels sprouts, will be needed to accompany it.

Metric	Imperial
25 g dripping	1 oz dripping
½ kg lean minced beef	1 lb lean minced beef
2 × 15 ml spoons flour	2 tablespoons flour
½ kg onions, peeled and quartered	1 lb onions, peeled and quartered
8 small pickled onions	8 small pickled onions
2 × 15 ml spoons tomato purée	2 tablespoons tomato purée
1 × 2.5 ml spoon sugar	½ teaspoon sugar
1 × 2.5 ml spoon dried thyme	½ teaspoon dried thyme
1 bay leaf, crushed	1 bay leaf, crushed
Salt and freshly ground black pepper	Salt and freshly ground black pepper
300 ml water	½ pint water
FOR THE CHEESE COBBLER:	FOR THE CHEESE COBBLER:
225 g self-raising flour	½ lb self-raising flour
1 × 2.5 ml spoon dry mustard	½ teaspoon dry mustard
Salt and freshly ground black pepper	Salt and freshly ground black pepper
40 g butter	1½ oz butter
75 g Cheddar cheese, finely grated	3 oz Cheddar cheese, finely grated
Few drops Tabasco sauce	Few drops Tabasco sauce
150 ml water	¼ pint water
1 × 15 ml spoon milk	1 tablespoon milk

Melt the dripping in a frying pan and lightly fry the minced beef until brown, stirring occasionally. Transfer the meat to a casserole, sprinkle with the flour and stir well. Add the quartered onions, pickled onions, tomato purée, sugar, herbs and seasoning to taste. Add the water or just sufficient water to cover the surface. Put the lid on the casserole and cook in a moderate oven (180°C/350°F or Gas Mark 4) for 1 hour.

To make the cheese cobbler sift the flour. Add the dry mustard and salt and pepper to taste to the sifted flour. Rub in the butter until the mixture resembles fine breadcrumbs, mix in the grated cheese and Tabasco, and blend to a soft dough with the water. Roll out on a floured surface until 1 cm/½ inch thick. Cut into rounds with a 7 cm/2½ inch fancy cutter, and arrange on top of the meat mixture overlapping in a decorative pattern. Brush the tops of the cobblers with the milk and return the uncovered casserole to the oven. Bake for a further 30 to 40 minutes or until golden.

Beefy cottage pie; Beef with cheese cobbler

Fidget pie

Fidget pie

An old country recipe from the Shires. Windfall apples were often used for it.

Metric

FOR THE PASTRY:
225 g flour
Pinch of salt
100 g lard cut into small pieces
2–3 × 15 ml spoons cold water

FOR THE FILLING:
1 large potato, peeled and chopped
1 large onion, peeled and chopped
¼ kg smoked streaky or collar bacon, diced
1 large cooking apple, peeled, cored and chopped
Salt and freshly ground black pepper
150 ml water
A little milk to glaze

Imperial

FOR THE PASTRY:
½ lb flour
Pinch of salt
¼ lb lard cut into small pieces
2–3 tablespoons cold water

FOR THE FILLING:
1 large potato, peeled and chopped
1 large onion, peeled and chopped
½ lb smoked streaky or collar bacon, diced
1 large cooking apple, peeled, cored and chopped
Salt and freshly ground black pepper
¼ pint water
A little milk to glaze

Sift the flour and salt into a bowl, add the lard and rub in with the fingertips until the mixture resembles fine breadcrumbs. Add enough cold water to mix to a stiff dough with a palette knife. Knead lightly on a floured surface for 1 minute until smooth. Wrap in foil or greaseproof paper and chill in the refrigerator for 30 minutes.

Grease a 1 litre / 1¾ pint pie dish and into it put layers of the chopped potato, chopped onion and lastly the diced bacon and chopped apple mixed, seasoning each layer well. Add the water.

Roll out the pastry fairly thickly, to fit the top of the pie dish, cutting a strip to go round the lip of the dish from the trimmings. Dampen the strip with cold water and put the pastry lid on top of this, pressing down well to seal. Cut two small steam vents in the lid. Decorate the top of the pie with the rest of the pastry trimmings. Brush with milk.

Bake in a fairly hot oven (200°C/400°F or Gas Mark 6) for about 30 minutes or until the pastry is golden-brown. Reduce the temperature to 160°C/325°F or Gas Mark 3 and cook for a further 1 hour, covering the pastry with foil, if necessary, to prevent it from becoming too brown. Serve hot.

Meat pie with potato crust

The mixture of two meats adds interest to this dish, with its
unusual crust. Pork is slightly cheaper than beef, which
saves a little on cost.

Metric
50 g dripping
1 large onion, peeled and
  chopped
Salt and freshly ground
  black pepper
1 × 15 ml spoon flour
½ kg stewing beef, diced
¼ kg lean pork, diced
1 small swede, peeled and
  diced
2 × 15 ml spoons orange
  juice
250 ml beef stock
FOR THE POTATO CRUST:
100 g self-raising flour
175 g potatoes, peeled,
  cooked and mashed
40 g shredded beef suet
Grated zest of 1 orange
Chopped parsley to garnish

Imperial
2 oz dripping
1 large onion, peeled and
  chopped
Salt and freshly ground
  black pepper
1 tablespoon flour
1 lb stewing beef, diced
½ lb lean pork, diced
1 small swede, peeled and
  diced
2 tablespoons orange juice
8 fl oz beef stock
FOR THE POTATO CRUST:
¼ lb self-raising flour
6 oz potatoes, peeled,
  cooked and mashed
1½ oz shredded beef suet
Grated zest of 1 orange
Chopped parsley to garnish

Meat pie with potato crust

Melt the dripping in a large frying pan and brown the
chopped onion in it. Season the flour and use to coat the
meat. Brown on all sides in the same fat. Transfer the onion
and meat mixture to a casserole, add the swede, orange
juice and stock which should just come to the level of the
contents. Cover the casserole and cook in a moderate oven
(180°C/350°F or Gas Mark 4) for 1 hour.

Meanwhile, prepare the potato crust by mixing together
the flour, mashed potatoes, suet, orange zest and seasoning
to taste. Knead lightly. Remove the lid from the casserole
and using it as a pattern, pat out the pastry with clean
floured hands to the shape of the casserole.

Stir the meat mixture, place the crust on top, making a
hole in the centre to allow the steam to escape. Replace the
lid and cook for a further 20 minutes. Garnish with chopped parsley.

49

Farmhouse turkey mould

Farmhouse turkey mould

Butchers often sell pigs' trotters cheaply because so few customers seem to want them. Yet the well-set jelly they produce helps to make a delicious meat mould for summer meals.

Metric	Imperial
2 pig's trotters	2 pig's trotters
Salt and freshly ground black pepper	Salt and freshly ground black pepper
4 portions boiling fowl or 2 turkey legs	4 portions boiling fowl or 2 turkey legs
¼ kg onions, peeled and chopped	½ lb onions, peeled and chopped
1 × 5 ml spoon dried sage	1 teaspoon dried sage

To pickle the pig's trotters, coat them in salt, place in a small basin, sprinkle with more salt and cover the basin. Refrigerate for 2 days.

Wash off all the salt, and place the trotters in a large saucepan with the portions of boiling fowl or the turkey legs, jointed to make 4 portions. Cover with cold water, season with salt and pepper, bring to the boil and skim carefully. Simmer, covered, for 2½ hours or until the meat is tender. Allow to cool.

Remove the trotters and poultry portions on to a clean enamel tray with a slotted draining spoon. Strip the meat from the bones and chop it roughly, discarding the bones and pieces of gristle. Pack the chopped meat into a pudding basin.

Bring the stock to the boil again, add the chopped onion and dried sage, and cook at a fast boil until the onion is tender and the stock reduced by about half. Strain, taste and adjust the seasoning if necessary. Pour just sufficient stock into the basin to cover the meat. (Any remaining stock can be used as the basis for a soup.) Allow to cool and refrigerate if possible overnight.

Turn out on to a serving dish, cut into wedges and surround with salad greens and radish roses.

Layered liver and bacon

This unusual method of cooking liver makes a change from serving it with boiled potatoes. It is just as good with ox liver.

Metric	Imperial
15 g lard	½ oz lard
½ kg pig's liver, thinly sliced	1 lb pig's liver, thinly sliced
4 rashers streaky bacon, rind removed	4 rashers streaky bacon, rind removed
2 medium-sized onions, peeled and chopped	2 medium-sized onions, peeled and chopped
2 medium-sized cooking apples, peeled, cored and chopped	2 medium-sized cooking apples, peeled, cored and chopped
1 × 5 ml spoon dried thyme	1 teaspoon dried thyme
1 × 15 ml spoon chopped parsley	1 tablespoon chopped parsley
Salt and freshly ground black pepper	Salt and freshly ground black pepper
8 × 15 ml spoons fresh white breadcrumbs	8 tablespoons fresh white breadcrumbs
300 ml hot water	½ pint hot water

Grease the inside of a casserole with the lard. Place half the sliced liver in a layer at the bottom and cover with 2 rashers of bacon. Mix together the chopped onion, apple, herbs and seasoning and place half the mixture over the bacon slices. Sprinkle half the breadcrumbs over it. Continue to fill the casserole with another layer each of liver, bacon and onion and apple mixture, finishing with the breadcrumbs. Pour in the hot water or just sufficient to cover the surface. Put the lid on the casserole and cook in a moderate oven (180°C/350°F or Gas Mark 4) for 1½ hours. Remove the lid, add a little more hot water if the contents appear too dry, and cook for another 30 minutes to allow the surface to brown.

Layered liver and bacon

Glazed lambs' tongues

Glazed lambs' tongues

This makes an impressive dish to serve as the main course for a cold buffet with various salads. The home-made glaze costs less than bought aspic jelly crystals. It also has a delicately spiced flavour which goes well with tongue. Any glaze left over may be set in a shallow dish, cut into tiny squares with a knife, and used as a garnish.

Metric	Imperial
4 lambs' tongues	*4 lambs' tongues*
4 cloves	*4 cloves*
1 small onion, peeled	*1 small onion, peeled*
1 × 5 ml spoon salt	*1 teaspoon salt*
1 bay leaf	*1 bay leaf*
1 × 2.5 cm piece of cinnamon stick	*1 × 1 inch piece of cinnamon stick*
3 × 15 ml spoons malt vinegar	*3 tablespoons malt vinegar*
4 small tomatoes	*4 small tomatoes*
1 × 15 ml spoon lemon juice	*1 tablespoon lemon juice*
1 × 5 ml spoon gelatine	*1 teaspoon gelatine*

Wash the tongues well in cold running water and place in a saucepan. Stick the cloves in the onion and add to the tongues together with the salt, bay leaf and cinnamon stick. Cover with cold water and bring to the boil. Put on the lid and simmer for 45 minutes. Add the vinegar and continue to simmer for a further 30 minutes. Take out the tongues, allow to cool, skin and remove any small bones from the cut ends.

Stand the tongues on their sides with their bases towards the centre, on a serving plate, and place the tomatoes between the tongues.

Strain 7 × 15 ml spoons/7 tablespoons of the cooking liquid into a small saucepan and add the lemon juice. Mix the gelatine with 2 × 15 ml spoons/2 tablespoons of the remaining cold stock and leave until it has softened and become spongy. Stir the softened gelatine into the liquid in the saucepan and heat until it has completely dissolved. Allow to cool and become syrupy.

Slowly spoon the setting glaze over the tongues and repeat several times to achieve a really good coating.

Serve green salad and either rice or potato salad.

Lambs' tongues with herb dumplings

As they are more trouble to prepare, lambs' tongues are usually cheaper than the equivalent weight in ox tongue, but have a very delicate flavour. If you use an ox tongue instead, the cooking time must be extended by 1 hour.

Metric	Imperial
4 small lambs' tongues	4 small lambs' tongues
1 × 15 ml spoon salt	1 tablespoon salt
2 large onions, peeled and sliced	2 large onions, peeled and sliced
1 bouquet garni	1 bouquet garni
25 g butter	1 oz butter
1 × 15 ml spoon flour	1 tablespoon flour
2 × 15 ml spoons capers	2 tablespoons capers
2 × 15 ml spoons lemon juice	2 tablespoons lemon juice
FOR THE DUMPLINGS:	FOR THE DUMPLINGS:
225 g self-raising flour	½ lb self-raising flour
100 g shredded beef suet	¼ lb shredded beef suet
1 × 2.5 ml spoon dried thyme	½ teaspoon dried thyme
Salt and freshly ground black pepper	Salt and freshly ground black pepper

Wash the tongues thoroughly. Put into a large saucepan, cover with water and add the salt. Bring to the boil, and drain. Cover the tongues with fresh water, add the sliced onion and bouquet garni, and bring to the boil. Reduce the heat, cover and simmer for 1¼ hours, or until the tongues are tender. Remove the tongues and leave to cool, then skin and take out any little bones. Cool the stock and skim off the fat from the surface. Remove the bouquet garni.

Melt the butter in a small saucepan and gradually stir in the flour. Cook for 2 minutes, stirring all the time. Add the stock (if necessary, make up to 450 ml / ¾ pint with boiling water), the capers and lemon juice. Continue stirring until the sauce has thickened.

Prepare the dumpling mixture by mixing together the flour, suet, thyme, seasoning and enough water to form a fairly stiff dough. Form the dough into about 12 round dumplings.

Dice the tongues, put into a casserole and cover with the sauce. Place the dumplings on top so that the surface is completely covered. Bake in a fairly hot oven (190°C/375°F or Gas Mark 5) for 30 minutes.

Lambs' tongues with herb dumplings

Baked stuffed hearts in cider

With careful cooking lambs' hearts can become really tender and succulent. A wooden cocktail stick can be used to secure the opening round the stuffing instead of thread.

Metric	Imperial
4 lambs' hearts	4 lambs' hearts
15 g butter or margarine	½ oz butter or margarine
1 small onion, peeled and finely chopped	1 small onion, peeled and finely chopped
50 g fresh white breadcrumbs	2 oz fresh white breadcrumbs
1 × 5 ml spoon dried mixed herbs	1 teaspoon dried mixed herbs
2 × 15 ml spoons seedless raisins	2 tablespoons seedless raisins
Salt and freshly ground black pepper	Salt and freshly ground black pepper
1 egg, beaten	1 egg, beaten
450 ml beef stock	¾ pint beef stock
150 ml dry cider	¼ pint dry cider
4 stalks celery, scrubbed and chopped	4 stalks celery, scrubbed and chopped
100 g carrots, peeled and chopped	¼ lb carrots, peeled and chopped

Trim the hearts and remove all blood vessels and membranes from the outside.

Melt the butter or margarine in a saucepan. Add the onion and cook gently until soft but not brown. Stir in the breadcrumbs, herbs, raisins and season to taste. Moisten with the beaten egg and use to stuff the hearts. Sew up the openings with a needle and white cotton thread.

Put the hearts into an ovenproof dish and pour over the stock and cider. Cover and cook in a warm oven (160°C/325°F or Gas Mark 3) for 1 hour. Add the chopped celery and carrots, cover and return to the oven for a further 1 hour, or until the hearts are tender. Serve with mashed potatoes.

Kidney in oriental sauce

This combination of flavours makes an almost exotic dish from a very nourishing and inexpensive variety of offal, ox kidney, which is usually combined with stewing beef in a pie or pudding.

Metric	Imperial
½ kg ox kidney	1 lb ox kidney
1 × 15 ml spoon vegetable oil	1 tablespoon vegetable oil
300 ml dry ginger ale	½ pint dry ginger ale
2 × 5 ml spoons malt vinegar	2 teaspoons malt vinegar
Salt and freshly ground black pepper	Salt and freshly ground black pepper
25 g butter	1 oz butter
100 g mushrooms, wiped and sliced	¼ lb mushrooms, wiped and sliced
25 g flaked almonds	1 oz flaked almonds
25 g sultanas	1 oz sultanas
1 × 15 ml spoon gravy powder	1 tablespoon gravy powder
3 × 15 ml spoons cold water	3 tablespoons cold water

Cut the ox kidney in slices about 2 cm / ¾ inch thick. Remove the core and chop the slices. Heat the vegetable oil in a saucepan and fry the pieces of kidney, turning several times, until lightly coloured all over, about 3 minutes. Add the ginger ale, vinegar and seasoning and bring to the boil. Simmer, covered, for 30 minutes. Meanwhile melt the butter in a frying pan and cook the sliced mushrooms for 3 minutes, turning frequently. Add the fried mushrooms, flaked almonds and sultanas to the kidney mixture, stir well and simmer for a further 10 minutes. Dissolve the gravy powder in the cold water and stir into the saucepan. Bring to the boil, stirring constantly. Simmer for a further 5 minutes. Taste and adjust the seasoning if necessary. Serve with boiled rice.

Kidney in oriental sauce

Baked stuffed hearts in cider

Rabbit in mustard sauce

TO GARNISH:
Chopped parsley
8 large bread croûtons
 fried in butter

TO GARNISH:
Chopped parsley
8 large bread croûtons
 fried in butter

On the day before you wish to serve the meal soak the rabbit joints for 2 hours in lightly salted water. Remove them and dry them well with absorbent kitchen paper. Coat the joints on all sides with the mustard and leave, covered, in the refrigerator overnight.

Coat the joints with the seasoned flour. Melt the butter in a flameproof casserole. Brown the joints on all sides, then add the diced salt pork, chopped onion and crushed garlic. Cover and cook for another 20 minutes, stirring occasionally. Then add the milk and seasoning and stir. Transfer the casserole to a warm oven (160°C/325°F or Gas Mark 3) and cook for another 45 minutes.

Place the rabbit joints on a heated serving dish, cover with the sauce from the casserole and garnish with chopped parsley and the fried bread croûtons.

Rabbit in mustard sauce

This casserole can be cooked entirely on top of the stove if preferred. Simmer very gently after adding the milk and test whether the rabbit is tender with a skewer after 45 minutes. It may take a little longer cooked this way.

Metric	Imperial
4 rabbit joints	*4 rabbit joints*
4 × 15 ml spoons French mustard	*4 tablespoons French mustard*
4 × 15 ml spoons seasoned flour for coating	*4 tablespoons seasoned flour for coating*
50 g butter	*2 oz butter*
50 g salt pork, rind removed and diced	*2 oz salt pork, rind removed and diced*
1 medium-sized onion, peeled and chopped	*1 medium-sized onion, peeled and chopped*
1 clove of garlic, crushed	*1 clove of garlic, crushed*
300 ml milk	*½ pint milk*
Salt and freshly ground black pepper	*Salt and freshly ground black pepper*

Pigeon casserole with grapes

When seedless grapes are reasonably priced and pigeons are in season, you may also be able to buy field mushrooms cheaply. They are excellent for this dish but must be peeled and carefully cleaned.

Metric	Imperial
25 g butter	*1 oz butter*
1 × 15 ml spoon vegetable oil	*1 tablespoon vegetable oil*
2 pigeons, split	*2 pigeons, split*
1 medium-sized onion, peeled and chopped	*1 medium-sized onion, peeled and chopped*
100 g button mushrooms, wiped and sliced	*¼ lb button mushrooms, wiped and sliced*
1 × 15 ml spoon flour	*1 tablespoon flour*
150 ml dry cider	*¼ pint dry cider*
150 ml strong chicken stock	*¼ pint strong chicken stock*
Salt and freshly ground black pepper	*Salt and freshly ground black pepper*
100 g seedless grapes	*¼ lb seedless grapes*
2 × 5 ml spoons cornflour	*2 teaspoons cornflour*
1 × 15 ml spoon water	*1 tablespoon water*

Melt the butter and oil together in a large heavy saucepan or flameproof casserole. Brown the pigeons quickly in the fat on both sides. Remove from the pan. Add the chopped onion to the fat and cook gently, covered, for a few minutes until soft. Add the sliced mushrooms, and fry for 2 minutes. Stir in the flour, cook for 1 minute, then add the cider, stock, seasoning to taste, and bring to the boil.

Return the pigeon halves to the pan, skin side down, and sprinkle the grapes round them. Cover and simmer for 1½ to 2 hours. Remove the pigeon halves and place, skin side up, on a warm serving dish.

Moisten the cornflour with the water, stir into the sauce and bring back to the boil. Cook gently for 3 minutes then pour over the pigeons.

Pigeons braised with cabbage

Pigeons which are too old for roasting become tender when braised with vegetables in a casserole, and have a richer flavour than younger birds. As a change, substitute orange zest and juice for the lemon.

Metric

2 × 15 ml spoons chicken
  fat, or butter
2 large pigeons, split
2 thick slices streaky
  bacon, rinds removed
  and chopped
2 large carrots, peeled and
  diced
1 large onion, peeled and
  chopped
Salt and freshly ground
  black pepper
1 medium-sized cabbage
  (¾–1 kg),
  trimmed and quartered
1 × 2.5 ml spoon ground
  bay leaves
1 chicken stock cube,
  crumbled
TO FINISH:
1 × 2.5 ml spoon grated
  lemon zest
1 × 15 ml spoon cornflour
2 × 15 ml spoons lemon
  juice

Imperial

2 tablespoons chicken fat,
  or butter
2 large pigeons, split
2 thick slices streaky
  bacon, rinds removed
  and chopped
2 large carrots, peeled and
  diced
1 large onion, peeled and
  chopped
Salt and freshly ground
  black pepper
1 medium-sized cabbage
  (1½–2 lb),
  trimmed and quartered
½ teaspoon ground bay
  leaves
1 chicken stock cube,
  crumbled
TO FINISH:
½ teaspoon grated lemon
  zest
1 tablespoon cornflour
2 tablespoons lemon juice

Pigeons braised with cabbage; Pigeon casserole with grapes

Heat the chicken fat or butter in a large, deep, flameproof casserole and sauté the pigeon halves in it, until lightly coloured on both sides. Remove and keep warm.

Fry the chopped bacon in the casserole until the fat begins to run, then add the diced carrot and chopped onion. Fry until just coloured, then return the pigeon halves to the casserole, breast side down, and season well. Surround with the cabbage quarters, add the ground bay leaves and the stock cube dissolved in 450 ml / ¾ pint boiling water. Bring to the boil. Cover closely, and simmer for 2 to 2½ hours or until the pigeons are tender. (Test with a fine skewer in the leg meat.)

Remove the vegetables and pigeon halves, breast side uppermost on to a warm serving dish with a slotted draining spoon. Add the grated lemon zest to the sauce. Boil for 1 to 2 minutes to reduce slightly.

Mix the cornflour with the lemon juice and stir into the sauce. Cook, stirring, over moderate heat for 3 minutes. Taste the sauce and adjust the seasoning if necessary. Spoon the sauce over the pigeon breasts. Serve with fluffy boiled rice or buttered noodles.

Fish, cheese and egg dishes

Many cooks feel that it is impossible to plan a good nourishing dish without meat. Here is help and encouragement, in the form of recipes for the other important high-protein providers, fish, cheese and eggs.

Fish varies in price according to the season, but from this collection of recipes using both fresh and canned fish you will be able to choose one that is economical.

Cheese remains marvellous value for money all round the year and the dishes suggested here could be varied using any kind of hard cheese. Those which crumble when grated are better for the recipes in which cheese is diced or chopped.

Eggs provide nourishing main dishes when combined with other ingredients. These recipes give you a choice of the useful basic soufflés, pancakes, omelettes and fritters, plus suggestions for variations.

Tomato and mackerel parcels

Metric	Imperial
4 fresh mackerel (about 350 g each)	4 fresh mackerel (about ¾ lb each)
Salt and freshly ground black pepper	Salt and freshly ground black pepper
4 spring onions, trimmed and sliced	4 spring onions, trimmed and sliced
4 large tomatoes, sliced	4 large tomatoes, sliced
1 lemon, quartered	1 lemon, quartered
1 bay leaf, quartered	1 bay leaf, quartered
1 × 5 ml spoon chopped parsley	1 teaspoon chopped parsley

Stuffed soused herrings; Tomato and mackerel parcels

Stuffed soused herrings

The unusual stuffing gives this old country favourite a new look and counteracts the richness of the herrings.

Metric	Imperial
5 herrings	5 herrings
Salt and freshly ground black pepper	Salt and freshly ground black pepper
1 small onion, peeled and cut into rings	1 small onion, peeled and cut into rings
1 small blade mace	1 small blade mace
3 cloves	3 cloves
8 peppercorns	8 peppercorns
150 ml water	¼ pint water
150 ml vinegar	¼ pint vinegar
FOR THE STUFFING:	FOR THE STUFFING:
50 g quick cook oats	2 oz quick cook oats
× 5 ml spoons chopped capers	2 teaspoons chopped capers
Grated zest of 1 small lemon	Grated zest of 1 small lemon
Salt and freshly ground black pepper	Salt and freshly ground black pepper
25 g butter, melted	1 oz butter, melted
1 egg, beaten	1 egg, beaten

Slit the mackerel from head to tail and clean them thoroughly. Remove the tails, fins, gills and eyes. The heads may also be removed if desired. Wash the fish well and dry on absorbent kitchen paper. Season the cavities.

Butter well 4 pieces of foil, each large enough to completely enclose a fish. Put on each square a layer of sliced onion and tomato, one mackerel, a lemon quarter and a piece of bay leaf. Season well, sprinkle with a little chopped parsley and fold up the foil, crimping the edges well together so that no juices can escape.

Place the 4 foil parcels on a baking sheet and bake in a moderate oven (180°C/350°F or Gas Mark 4) for 20 minutes. Serve individually in the foil parcels.

Clean and bone the herrings and lay them flat, skin side down. Sprinkle with salt and pepper.

To make the stuffing, place the oats, chopped capers, lemon zest and seasoning to taste in a bowl. Add the melted butter and beaten egg and mix thoroughly. The mixture should be stiff but not unmanageable. Add a little milk if necessary. Put equal quantities of the oat stuffing near the tail end of each herring, then roll up from the tail end.

Arrange the stuffed herrings, joins downwards, in a single layer in an ovenproof dish with the onion rings, mace, cloves and peppercorns. Mix together the water and vinegar and pour over the herrings. Bake in a fairly hot oven (190°C/375°F or Gas Mark 5) for 30 to 35 minutes. Serve hot or cold accompanied by a green salad.

Fish in pastry envelopes

Cooked white fish in a creamy sauce tucked inside crispy oat pastry makes a change from the usual fish pie.

Metric
225 g flour
100 g quick cook oats
Pinch of salt
175 g margarine
4–5 × 15 ml spoons cold water
1 egg, beaten
Quick cook oats for sprinkling
FOR THE FILLING:
25 g butter
1 × 15 ml spoon flour
150 ml milk
1 × 15 ml spoon chopped parsley
350 g white fish fillets
Salt and freshly ground black pepper

Imperial
½ lb flour
¼ lb quick cook oats
Pinch of salt
6 oz margarine
4–5 tablespoons cold water
1 egg, beaten
Quick cook oats for sprinkling
FOR THE FILLING:
1 oz butter
1 tablespoon flour
¼ pint milk
1 tablespoon chopped parsley
¾ lb white fish fillets
Salt and freshly ground black pepper

First make the filling. Melt the butter in a small saucepan. Stir in the flour and cook for 1 minute. Gradually stir in the milk and bring to the boil, stirring constantly. Add the parsley and cook for 2 minutes, stirring all the time.

Cut the fish into bite-sized pieces and place in a bowl with the parsley sauce and seasoning to taste. Mix thoroughly and allow to become cold.

Meanwhile, make the pastry. Mix together the flour, oats and salt in a bowl. Rub in the margarine and bind with cold water to give a stiff consistency. Roll out the pastry on a floured surface to a rectangle about 25 × 38 cm / 10 × 15 inches and divide into six 12.5 cm / 5 inch squares. Place equal quantities of the fish mixture in the centre of each pastry square. Brush the edges of the pastry with water and join the edges together to form envelopes. Brush each envelope with beaten egg and sprinkle with extra oats. Place on a lightly greased baking sheet and bake in a fairly hot oven (200°C/400°F or Gas Mark 6) for 10 minutes, then reduce the heat to cool (150°C/300°F or Gas Mark 2) and cook a further 20 to 25 minutes.
Makes 6

Fish in pastry envelopes

Family fish pie

The skin can be removed after cooking if preferred but some cooks believe it adds to the flavour of the milk stock.

Metric	Imperial
1 kg coley or other white fish, skinned	*2 lb coley or other white fish, skinned*
600 ml milk	*1 pint milk*
50 g butter	*2 oz butter*
50 g flour	*2 oz flour*
2 hard-boiled eggs, shelled and roughly chopped	*2 hard-boiled eggs, shelled and roughly chopped*
Salt and freshly ground black pepper	*Salt and freshly ground black pepper*
225 g frozen peas, defrosted	*½ lb frozen peas, defrosted*
1 kg freshly cooked potatoes, mashed	*2 lb freshly cooked potatoes, mashed*

Place the fish in a saucepan, cover with the milk and poach for 10 minutes. Lift out the fish with a slotted draining spoon, remove the bones and flake the fish. Reserve the milk for the sauce.

Heat the butter in a saucepan, stir in the flour and cook for 2 minutes. Gradually add the milk and bring to the boil stirring constantly. Remove from the heat. Stir in the flaked fish and chopped eggs and season to taste. Pour the mixture into a buttered baking dish. Cover with the defrosted peas and spread the mashed potatoes over the top. Bake in a fairly hot oven (200°C/400°F or Gas Mark 6) for 30 minutes, or until golden-brown on top.
Serves 6 to 8

Family fish pie

Pilchard and potato cakes

Pilchards are often neglected in favour of more expensive canned fish, but combine very well with potatoes to make a piping hot supper dish.

Metric	Imperial
225 g freshly cooked potatoes, mashed	½ lb freshly cooked potatoes, mashed
1 × 225 g can pilchards in tomato sauce, boned and flaked	1 × 8 oz can pilchards in tomato sauce, boned and flaked
1 × 5 ml spoon salt	1 teaspoon salt
Freshly ground black pepper	Freshly ground black pepper
1 × 2.5 ml spoon finely grated onion	½ teaspoon finely grated onion
1 × 2.5 ml spoon lemon juice	½ teaspoon lemon juice
FOR COATING:	FOR COATING:
1 egg, beaten	1 egg, beaten
75 g dried breadcrumbs	3 oz dried breadcrumbs
Vegetable oil for frying	Vegetable oil for frying

Dry mash the potatoes (without adding any milk or butter) and place in a bowl with the fish, seasoning, grated onion and lemon juice. Combine gently with a fork until the mixture holds together. Shape into 8 round flat cakes on a floured board. Dip the cakes into the beaten egg, making sure that they are evenly covered, then coat with breadcrumbs.

Heat the oil gently in a deep-fat fryer or saucepan until it is hot enough to turn a stale bread cube golden in 20 to 30 seconds (180–190°C/350–375°F). Lower the cakes, 4 at a time, into the hot oil and fry for 1 to 2 minutes until crisp and golden-brown on all sides. Drain on absorbent kitchen paper.

The fish cakes may also be shallow fried for 2 to 3 minutes on each side or until golden-brown.
Makes 8 cakes

Cod and bean pie; Pilchard and potato cakes

Cod and bean pie

This recipe offers a change from the usual fish pie topped with mashed potato. The result is equally good if coley is substituted for cod.

Metric	Imperial
175 g haricot beans, soaked overnight in cold water	6 oz haricot beans, soaked overnight in cold water
2 medium-sized onions, peeled and chopped	2 medium-sized onions, peeled and chopped
1 kg cod or other white fish fillet, skinned and cut into small pieces	2 lb cod or other white fish fillet, skinned and cut into small pieces
4 rashers streaky bacon, cut into strips	4 rashers streaky bacon, cut into strips
Salt and freshly ground black pepper	Salt and freshly ground black pepper
Pinch of dried thyme	Pinch of dried thyme
Pinch of dried marjoram	Pinch of dried marjoram
600 ml milk or milk and fish stock mixed	1 pint milk or milk and fish stock mixed
½ kg potatoes, peeled and very thinly sliced	1 lb potatoes, peeled and very thinly sliced
25 g butter	1 oz butter
1 × 15 ml spoon chopped parsley to garnish	1 tablespoon chopped parsley to garnish

Drain the haricot beans, cover with fresh cold water, bring to the boil and simmer for 1½ hours or until tender. Drain.

Put the onions into a greased casserole and cover with the fish and strips of bacon. Season to taste and add the herbs. Add a layer of cooked beans and pour in the milk or milk and stock. Top with the potatoes which should overlap and be arranged to form an attractive crust.

Dot the pie with butter and bake in a moderate oven (180°C/350°F or Gas Mark 4) for about 40 minutes or until the potatoes are cooked and golden-brown. Scatter the chopped parsley over the pie and serve very hot.
Serves 6

Crispy corned tuna

Sardine eggs

Crispy corned tuna

Almost all the ingredients for this crispy-topped pie come from the store cupboard, and it takes less than half an hour to prepare and cook.

Metric	Imperial
25 g butter	1 oz butter
25 g flour	1 oz flour
300 ml milk	½ pint milk
50 g Cheddar cheese, grated	2 oz Cheddar cheese, grated
Salt and freshly ground black pepper	Salt and freshly ground black pepper
1 × 200 g can tuna fish	1 × 7 oz can tuna fish
1 × 326 g can sweetcorn	1 × 11½ oz can sweetcorn
2 large tomatoes, finely sliced	2 large tomatoes, finely sliced
1 × 71 g packet salted potato crisps	1 × 2½ oz packet salted potato crisps

Melt the butter in a saucepan. Stir in the flour and cook for 1 minute. Gradually add the milk and bring to the boil, stirring constantly. Simmer for 2 minutes, stir in the cheese and season to taste. Flake the tuna and add to the sauce with the liquid from the can. Fold in the drained sweetcorn.

Use the tomato slices to line a greased ovenproof dish. Spoon the tuna mixture into the centre of the dish and crumble the potato crisps on top. Place in a moderate oven (180°C/350°F or Gas Mark 4) for about 20 minutes, until the top is brown and crisp. Serve with thick slices of french bread.

Sardine eggs

Whether served as a starter, high tea or supper dish all the family will enjoy these stuffed eggs.

Metric	Imperial
4 eggs, hard-boiled and shelled	4 eggs, hard-boiled and shelled
1 × 124 g can sardines in oil, drained	1 × 4⅜ oz can sardines in oil, drained
1 × 5 ml spoon chopped parsley	1 teaspoon chopped parsley
2 × 5 ml spoons quick cook oats	2 teaspoons quick cook oats
2 × 15 ml spoons single cream	2 tablespoons single cream
Pinch of cayenne pepper	Pinch of cayenne pepper
Salt and freshly ground black pepper	Salt and freshly ground black pepper
TO FINISH:	TO FINISH:
Lettuce leaves	Lettuce leaves
Parsley sprigs	Parsley sprigs

Cut each egg in half lengthwise. Using a teaspoon carefully remove the yolks and place them in a basin. Add the sardines to the egg yolks with the parsley, oats, cream and cayenne pepper. Mash with a fork then beat thoroughly until smooth and well blended. Season to taste and divide the mixture equally among the egg halves.

Place the stuffed eggs on a bed of lettuce leaves and garnish with parsley sprigs. Serve with brown bread and butter.

Leek and bacon gratin

A minute or two under a hot grill gives a beautiful golden-brown finish to this economical yet satisfying supper dish.

Metric
8 large leeks, white and
   pale green part washed
   and sliced into 5 cm
   lengths
1 large carrot, peeled and
   sliced into 5 cm lengths
12 rashers streaky bacon
FOR THE SAUCE:
25 g butter
25 g flour
300 ml milk
Salt and freshly ground
   black pepper
50 g Cheddar cheese,
   grated

Imperial
8 large leeks, white and
   pale green part washed
   and sliced into 2 inch
   lengths
1 large carrot, peeled and
   sliced into 2 inch lengths
12 rashers streaky bacon
FOR THE SAUCE:
1 oz butter
1 oz flour
½ pint milk
Salt and freshly ground
   black pepper
2 oz Cheddar cheese,
   grated

TO FINISH:
50 g Cheddar cheese,
   grated
50 g fresh white
   breadcrumbs

TO FINISH:
2 oz Cheddar cheese,
   grated
2 oz fresh white
   breadcrumbs

Cook the sliced leeks and carrots in boiling, salted water to cover for 10 to 15 minutes or until tender. Drain, reserving the liquid and turn into a buttered flameproof casserole.

Meanwhile prepare the sauce. Melt the butter in a pan, stir in the flour and cook for 2 to 3 minutes, stirring constantly. Remove the pan from the heat and gradually add the milk and 150 ml/¼ pint of the liquid from the vegetables, stirring constantly. Return the pan to the heat. Bring slowly to the boil stirring all the time. Lower the heat, add the seasoning to taste and simmer gently until the sauce thickens. Stir in the 50 g/2 oz cheese.

Grill the bacon rashers, arrange on top of the leeks and carrots and cover with the sauce. Sprinkle thickly with the mixed cheese and breadcrumbs. Pour over the drippings from the grilled bacon and place the dish under a hot grill until the surface is golden-brown and crisp. Serve immediately.

Leek and bacon gratin

Cheese and onion pudding

For young children or invalids, the onions may be omitted to give a very delicate savoury cheese pudding.

Metric	Imperial
25 g butter	1 oz butter
2 medium-sized onions, peeled and finely sliced	2 medium-sized onions, peeled and finely sliced
600 ml milk	1 pint milk
100 g soft white breadcrumbs	¼ lb soft white breadcrumbs
100 g Cheddar cheese, grated	¼ lb Cheddar cheese, grated
Salt and freshly ground black pepper	Salt and freshly ground black pepper
3 large eggs, lightly beaten	3 large eggs, lightly beaten

Heat the butter in a pan. Add the onions and fry gently until golden. Add the milk and bring just to boiling point. Pour over the breadcrumbs, stir well. Fold in the cheese, seasoning and beaten eggs. Turn into a greased pie dish and bake in a fairly hot oven (190°C/375°F or Gas Mark 5) for 30 minutes or until golden-brown and well risen. Serve immediately.

Cheese and potato pasties

These pasties may be eaten hot or cold and are ideal for picnics and packed lunches.

Metric	Imperial
225 g flour	½ lb flour
Pinch of salt	Pinch of salt
100 g lard, cut into pieces	¼ lb lard, cut into pieces
2–3 × 15 ml spoons cold water	2–3 tablespoons cold water
FOR THE FILLING:	FOR THE FILLING:
2 medium-sized potatoes, peeled and chopped	2 medium-sized potatoes, peeled and chopped
1 × 5 ml spoon grated onion	1 teaspoon grated onion
100 g Cheddar cheese, diced	¼ lb Cheddar cheese, diced
Salt and freshly ground black pepper	Salt and freshly ground black pepper
Pinch of dried sage (optional)	Pinch of dried sage (optional)

Sift the flour and salt into a bowl. Rub in the lard until the mixture resembles fine breadcrumbs. Stir in just sufficient water to hold the mixture together, then form into a smooth ball. Wrap in foil or greaseproof paper and chill in the refrigerator for 30 minutes.

Roll out the pastry on a floured surface and cut out 4 rounds using a saucer. Mix the filling ingredients together and place an equal amount in the centre of each circle. Dampen the edges, draw the opposite edges together over the centres and pinch firmly together to seal.

Place the pasties on a greased baking sheet and bake in a fairly hot oven (200°C/400°F or Gas Mark 6) for 30 minutes. Serve hot or cold.

Egg croquettes

These delicately flavoured croquettes make a tasty luncheon or supper dish. They are particularly suitable when a meal without meat is called for.

Metric	Imperial
4 hard-boiled eggs, shelled and chopped	4 hard-boiled eggs, shelled and chopped
1 egg yolk	1 egg yolk
Salt and freshly ground pepper	Salt and freshly ground pepper
FOR THE PANADA:	FOR THE PANADA:
250 ml milk	8 fl oz milk
1 slice of onion	1 slice of onion
3 peppercorns	3 peppercorns
1 blade of mace	1 blade of mace
1 small bay leaf	1 small bay leaf
50 g butter	2 oz butter
50 g flour	2 oz flour
FOR COATING:	FOR COATING:
Seasoned flour	Seasoned flour
1 egg, beaten	1 egg, beaten
Dry white breadcrumbs	Dry white breadcrumbs
Vegetable oil for frying	Vegetable oil for frying

First make the panada. Put the milk into a saucepan. Add the onion, peppercorns, mace and bay leaf. Bring slowly to the boil then remove from the heat, cover and allow to stand for 10 minutes. Strain and discard the flavourings.

Melt the butter in a clean saucepan over low heat. Stir in the flour and allow to cook for 3 minutes stirring constantly. Gradually add the flavoured milk and bring to the boil, stirring all the time. The mixture should be very thick. Remove from the heat and add the chopped hard-boiled eggs, egg yolk and seasoning to taste. Turn the mixture out on a plate to cool then chill well.

Shape into 8 croquettes and coat with the seasoned flour. Dip into the beaten egg and cover evenly with breadcrumbs.

Heat the oil in a deep-fat fryer or saucepan until it is hot enough to turn a stale bread cube golden-brown in 30 seconds (190°C/375°F). Fry the croquettes, 4 at a time, in the hot oil, until golden-brown and crisp. Drain on absorbent kitchen paper and serve hot with a tomato sauce.
Makes 8

(clockwise) Cheese and potato pasties; Egg croquettes; Cheese and onion pudding; Tomato sauce (see page 137)

'Pennywise' pancakes

This pancake batter is very economical. You can make it a little richer by using two eggs and all milk instead of milk and water.

Metric	Imperial
100 g plain flour	*¼ lb plain flour*
1 egg	*1 egg*
150 ml milk	*¼ pint milk*
150 ml water	*¼ pint water*
1 × 15 ml spoon vegetable oil	*1 tablespoon vegetable oil*
Vegetable oil for frying	*Vegetable oil for frying*

To make up the batter, place the flour, egg, milk, water and oil in a bowl and whisk vigorously until smooth.

Heat a little oil in a pancake pan, add about 2 × 15 ml spoons / 2 tablespoons of the batter and swirl it round the pan to coat the base evenly. Cook until the top surface just becomes set and dry then toss or flip the pancake over using a palette knife and cook the other side until golden.

Slip the cooked pancake on to a warm serving plate and keep hot. Add a little more oil to the pan before cooking each pancake and continue until all the batter has been used. If cooking in a non-stick pan you may not require to add any more oil. Serve sprinkled with caster sugar and lemon juice.

Makes 8

Satsuma butter pancakes

Finely grate the zest from 2 satsumas and work into 50g/2oz softened unsalted butter with 50g/2oz sifted icing sugar and 1×5ml spoon/1 teaspoon undiluted orange squash. Spread this satsuma butter thinly over 8 hot pancakes. Fold each one in half, then in half again and arrange on a warm serving dish. Sprinkle generously with sifted icing sugar and place under a fairly hot grill until reheated. Serve decorated with thin strips of orange rind. (The satsuma segments, with the pith and membranes carefully removed, can be added to a fruit salad.)

Satsuma butter pancakes; 'Pennywise' pancake; Rolled pancakes with dressed crab

Rolled pancakes with dressed crab

Mix the contents of a 50g/1¾oz can of dressed crab with butter and 150ml/¼ pint Savoury white sauce (see page 30) until well blended. Stir in 1×15ml spoon/1 tablespoon chopped parsley. Divide the mixture among 8 hot cooked pancakes and roll them up round the filling. Arrange closely packed in a shallow ovenproof dish, sprinkle with 50g/2oz grated cheese and place under a hot grill until the cheese melts.

Basic omelette

For a light meal, an omelette made with two eggs is sufficient to serve one person; with a filling and a salad on the side it becomes quite a substantial dish. The classic 17.5 cm/7 inch pan makes a two-egg omelette of just the right thickness. As each one takes only about 2 minutes to cook, and it is rather difficult to prepare a larger omelette to be divided into portions successfully, this is the recommended method.

Metric	Imperial
2 eggs	*2 eggs*
1 × 15 ml spoon cold water	*1 tablespoon cold water*
Salt and freshly ground	*Salt and freshly ground*
* black pepper*	* black pepper*
Butter for frying	*Butter for frying*

Beat the eggs lightly together in a small bowl, stir in the water and season to taste.

Melt just sufficient butter in the omelette pan to coat the base well. When the butter starts to foam, pour in the egg mixture all at once and tilt the pan so that it coats the base evenly. If necessary, use a palette knife to lift the edges away from the side and allow any unset mixture to run underneath. (If you use a non-stick pan, stir the egg mixture as it begins to set instead of tilting the pan.)

When the top of the omelette is almost set but still creamy, hold the pan over a warm plate and turn the omelette over away from the handle on to the plate, folding it in half or into three. Serve at once as the egg continues to cook in its own heat and the omelette may become leathery if kept waiting.
Serves 1

Omelette with croûtons
Trim one slice of white bread and cut into dice. Melt 1 × 15 ml spoon/1 tablespoon bacon fat in the omelette pan and use to fry the bread dice until golden-brown. Add a little butter and the omelette mixture and cook as for Basic omelette. Serve sprinkled with chopped mixed fresh herbs (parsley, chives, marjoram).

Omelette with baked bean stuffing
Peel and very finely chop one small onion. Melt 15 g/½ oz butter in a small saucepan and use to fry the onion until soft. Stir in 2 × 15 ml spoons/2 tablespoons baked beans in tomato sauce and a few drops of Tabasco sauce. Leave over gentle heat while you cook the omelette. Spoon the filling into the centre of the omelette and fold over on to a warm plate.

Basic omelette; Omelette with croûtons; Omelette with baked bean stuffing

Basic savoury fritters

For light meals this type of fritter makes a tasty change from such dishes as macaroni cheese. They are delicious served quite simply sprinkled with cheese or the batter can be combined with small quantities of more expensive ingredients, using it as an extender.

Metric	Imperial
50g plain flour	2 oz plain flour
1 × 1.25 ml spoon salt	¼ teaspoon salt
1 egg	1 egg
15g butter, melted	½ oz butter, melted
100 ml flat beer	4 fl oz flat beer
1 egg white	1 egg white
Vegetable oil for frying	Vegetable oil for frying

Sift the flour and salt into a bowl. Beat the egg lightly and stir in the melted butter. Pour this mixture into the flour with the beer and beat until just smooth. Allow the batter to stand at room temperature for 1 hour if you have time. Stiffly whisk the egg white and fold into the batter.

Heat the oil in a deep-fat fryer or saucepan until it is hot enough to turn a stale bread cube golden in 30 seconds (190°C/375°F). Drop spoonfuls (1 × 15 ml spoon/1 table-spoon) of the mixture into the hot oil, a few at a time, and fry until crisp and golden-brown. Remove and drain on absorbent kitchen paper. Transfer to a warm serving dish and serve hot, sprinkled with crumbled Danish blue or grated hard cheese.

Salami fritters
Remove the rind and finely chop 75 g/3 oz Continental sausage (Salami, Mortadella or Cervelat). Stir this into the basic batter, drop by spoonfuls and fry as Basic savoury fritters.

Chicken fritters
Very finely chop 100 g/¼ lb cooked chicken. Stir into the basic batter with 1 × 15 ml spoon/1 tablespoon grated mild onion and a little freshly ground black pepper. Drop by spoonfuls and fry as Basic savoury fritters.

Banana fritters; Apple fritters (right)

Chicken fritters; Salami fritters (above)

Basic sweet fritters

Fritters which are carefully cooked in hot oil are dry and crisp, need little draining and are therefore not extravagant in wasting cooking oil.

Metric	Imperial
100 g plain flour	¼ lb plain flour
1 × 5 ml spoon baking powder	1 teaspoon baking powder
1 × 2.5 ml spoon salt	½ teaspoon salt
2 × 15 ml spoons sugar	2 tablespoons sugar
2 eggs, separated	2 eggs, separated
2 × 15 ml spoons water	2 tablespoons water
Vegetable oil for frying	Vegetable oil for frying

Sift the flour, baking powder and salt into a bowl and stir in the sugar. Lightly whisk the egg yolks and water and stir into the dry ingredients. Beat until smooth. Stiffly whisk the egg whites and fold into the mixture.

Heat the oil in a deep-fat fryer or saucepan until it is hot enough to turn a stale bread cube golden-brown in 45 seconds (185°C/360°F). Drop spoonfuls (1 × 5 ml spoon/ 1 teaspoon) of the mixture into the hot oil, a few at a time, and fry until crisp and golden-brown. Remove and drain on absorbent kitchen paper. Transfer to a warm dish and serve hot, with a sweet sauce and sprinkled with sifted icing sugar.

Apple fritters
Peel, core and thinly slice 2 large dessert apples. Dip the apple slices into the batter and fry until golden-brown.

Banana fritters
Peel and thinly slice 2 large ripe, but firm, bananas. Stir gently into the batter and drop by spoonfuls (1 × 15 ml spoon/1 tablespoon) into the hot oil. Fry until golden-brown.

Cheese soufflé

Although many cooks hesitate to attempt a soufflé under the mistaken impression that it is expensive and difficult to make, the only essential is that it must be served straight from oven to table and simply cannot be kept waiting.

Metric	Imperial
40 g butter	1½ oz butter
2 × 15 ml spoons flour	2 tablespoons flour
300 ml hot milk	½ pint hot milk
4 eggs, separated	4 eggs, separated
100 g Cheddar cheese, grated	¼ lb Cheddar cheese, grated
Salt and freshly ground black pepper	Salt and freshly ground black pepper
Pinch of grated nutmeg	Pinch of grated nutmeg

Melt the butter in a saucepan. Add the flour and stir over moderate heat for 1 minute. Gradually add the milk and bring to the boil, stirring constantly. Cook for 2 minutes. Remove from the heat, and beat in the egg yolks one at a time. Stir in the cheese and the seasonings. Replace over heat and stir constantly for 1 minute. Stiffly whisk the egg whites, remove the pan from the heat and fold a little egg white into the cheese mixture. Quickly but thoroughly fold in the rest of the egg white, making sure that all the cheese mixture at the bottom of the saucepan is blended in. Have ready a 15 cm/6 inch soufflé dish, well buttered. If liked, sprinkle a little extra grated cheese into the base of the soufflé dish. Turn the mixture into it and bake in a fairly hot oven (200°C/400°F or Gas Mark 6) for about 25 minutes, or until golden-brown and just firm.

Cheese soufflé

Fresh vegetables and salads in season

Unusual vegetable dishes are particularly useful in winter when the choice is often limited to root vegetables, and these become rather boring when repeatedly presented in the same form. By combining two root vegetables in one dish, more interesting results can be obtained and the necessity to provide potatoes as well is often avoided.

Since the tendency is to think of salads in terms of lettuce and cucumber only, perhaps garnished with tomatoes and a bottled dressing, there are lots of new ideas included here which are well worth trying. In fact, one new recipe for every month of the year, so that you can always make use of vegetables in season for your salads. These colourful additions to the usual menu can be served on the side, or become a main dish in themselves with a selection of sliced cold meats and sausages.

Home-made dressings give an exciting new touch to even the simplest salad. One is given based on yogurt and the other a delicate wine vinaigrette.

Spiced carrots and swede

When the long winter season makes everyone bored with root vegetables, it is useful to be able to present them in new disguises. Here, the combination of flavours is irresistible.

Metric	Imperial
4 large carrots, peeled and sliced	4 large carrots, peeled and sliced
½ kg swede, peeled and diced	1 lb swede, peeled and diced
25 g butter, melted	1 oz butter, melted
2 × 15 ml spoons orange juice	2 tablespoons orange juice
1 × 5 ml spoon grated orange zest	1 teaspoon grated orange zest
Good pinch of ground ginger	Good pinch of ground ginger
Good pinch of grated nutmeg	Good pinch of grated nutmeg
Salt and freshly ground black pepper	Salt and freshly ground black pepper

Place the sliced carrots and diced swede in an ovenproof dish.

Combine the melted butter, orange juice, grated orange zest, ground ginger and grated nutmeg and seasoning to taste. Pour over the vegetables.

Lightly cover with foil and bake in a fairly hot oven (190°C/375°F or Gas Mark 5) for 45 minutes.

NOTE: Potatoes can be peeled, sliced and baked in seasoned milk in a similar dish on the same shelf of the oven. Both dishes should then be ready to serve at the same time.

Vegetable curry of your choice

Serve this filling vegetable curry with hard-boiled eggs to turn it into a main dish. For good measure put some appetizing curry accompaniments on the table: mango or peach chutney, sliced banana sprinkled with lemon juice and dessicated coconut and chopped fresh mint leaves in yogurt.

Metric	Imperial
1 × 15 ml spoon turmeric	1 tablespoon turmeric
1 × 15 ml spoon flour	1 tablespoon flour
1 kg mixed fresh vegetables, prepared and cut into suitable pieces, eg. cauliflower sprigs, sliced beans, carrots, celery, courgettes, green or red peppers, potatoes	2 lb mixed fresh vegetables, prepared and cut into suitable pieces, eg. cauliflower sprigs, sliced beans, carrots, celery, courgettes, green or red peppers, potatoes
4 × 15 ml spoons vegetable oil or 50 g dripping, for frying	4 tablespoons vegetable oil or 2 oz dripping, for frying
3 medium-sized onions, peeled and chopped	3 medium-sized onions, peeled and chopped
2 medium-sized cooking apples, peeled, cored and chopped	2 medium-sized cooking apples, peeled, cored and chopped
2 × 15 ml spoons curry powder	2 tablespoons curry powder
1 × 396 g can tomatoes	1 × 14 oz can tomatoes
1 × 5 ml spoon ground coriander	1 teaspoon ground coriander
¼ kg haricot or red kidney beans or chick peas or a combination of these, soaked overnight and cooked	½ lb haricot or red kidney beans or chick peas or a combination of these, soaked overnight and cooked
Salt	Salt
3 hard-boiled eggs, shelled and halved, to finish (optional)	3 hard-boiled eggs, shelled and halved, to finish (optional)

Mix the turmeric and flour together in a large bowl. Put in the prepared fresh vegetables and toss to coat lightly with the mixture.

Heat the oil or dripping in a large frying or sauté pan. Add the fresh vegetables and fry for 3 to 4 minutes. Remove from the pan with a slotted draining spoon and set aside.

Add the chopped onion and apple to the fat remaining in the pan and fry gently for 5 minutes. Stir in the curry powder and continue frying for a further 3 minutes. Pour in the tomatoes and their liquid, add the coriander, mixed vegetables and the cooked beans or chick peas. Add salt to taste and bring to the boil. Cover and simmer for 30 minutes or until the vegetables are tender. Stir occasionally to prevent the curry powder from sticking and, if the sauce becomes too thick, add a little water.

Just before serving add the hard-boiled eggs and heat through.

Vegetable curry of your choice; Spiced carrots and swede

Fruited beetroot dice; Turnip and potato purée

Fruited beetroot dice

Beetroot is rarely offered as a hot vegetable but with a simple savoury white sauce, or served as in this recipe combined with fruit juice, it makes a change from the usual winter root vegetables.

Metric	Imperial
1 × 15 ml spoon soft brown sugar	1 tablespoon soft brown sugar
75 ml pineapple juice	3 fl oz pineapple juice
1 × 15 ml spoon white vinegar	1 tablespoon white vinegar
1 × 15 ml spoon cornflour	1 tablespoon cornflour
15 g butter	½ oz butter
Salt and freshly ground black pepper	Salt and freshly ground black pepper
½ kg cooked beetroot, peeled and finely diced	1 lb cooked beetroot, peeled and finely diced
1 × 15 ml spoon finely chopped spring onion to garnish	1 tablespoon finely chopped spring onion to garnish

Place the sugar, pineapple juice, vinegar and cornflour in a small saucepan. Stir until smooth then bring to the boil, stirring constantly. Reduce the heat and simmer for 2 minutes, stirring occasionally. Beat in the butter and season to taste.

Fold the beetroot dice into the sauce and reheat carefully to boiling point. Spoon into a warm serving dish and garnish with the chopped spring onion.

Turnip and potato purée

This old-fashioned method of combining two favourite winter root vegetables is known in Sussex as 'potato pond'. The melting butter in each serving gives it a luxury touch.

Metric	Imperial
40 g butter	1½ oz butter
350 g young turnips, peeled and sliced	¾ lb young turnips, peeled and sliced
350 g potatoes, peeled and sliced	¾ lb potatoes, peeled and sliced
1 small onion, peeled and sliced	1 small onion, peeled and sliced
Salt and freshly ground black pepper	Salt and freshly ground black pepper
300 ml milk	½ pint milk
1 × 2.5 ml spoon grated nutmeg	½ teaspoon grated nutmeg
25 g butter to finish	1 oz butter to finish

Heat the butter in a saucepan until just melted, add the sliced turnip, potato and onion. Sauté the vegetables, stirring frequently, for 3 minutes. Season to taste, add the milk and sprinkle in the grated nutmeg. Bring to the boil, reduce the heat, cover and cook gently for 10 minutes or until the vegetables are tender. Liquidize in an electric blender or pass through a sieve. Return the purée to the saucepan and reheat.

Spoon on to individual plates, and mound up each serving. Make a dent in the top of each mound with the back of a spoon and put in a knob of butter.

Spicy red cabbage; Sautéed vegetable marrow

Spicy red cabbage

This vegetable is almost a meal in itself when cooked in this continental style and makes the perfect partner to roast pork or a bacon joint.

Metric	Imperial
1 kg red cabbage, core removed and finely shredded	2 lb red cabbage, core removed and finely shredded
½ kg onions, peeled and finely chopped	1 lb onions, peeled and finely chopped
½ kg cooking apples, peeled, cored and finely chopped	1 lb cooking apples, peeled, cored and finely chopped
Salt and freshly ground black pepper	Salt and freshly ground black pepper
Good pinch of ground mixed spice	Good pinch of ground mixed spice
2 × 15 ml spoons soft brown sugar	2 tablespoons soft brown sugar
2 × 15 ml spoons wine vinegar	2 tablespoons wine vinegar
25 g butter	1 oz butter

Put a layer of shredded cabbage in the bottom of a casserole. Arrange a layer of chopped onions and apples over the top. Season and add a little mixed spice and a sprinkling of sugar. Fill up the dish with alternating layers of onion and apple mixture and cabbage, seasoning each layer and sprinkling with the spices and sugar. Pour in the wine vinegar and dot the surface with the butter. Cover and bake in a cool oven (150°C/300°F or Gas Mark 2) for 2 hours.

Sautéed vegetable marrow

When boiled in water marrow loses all its delicate flavour, but if cooked by this conservative method it has a good texture and combines well with a hint of onion and herbs.

Metric	Imperial
40 g butter	1½ oz butter
1 × 15 ml spoon vegetable oil	1 tablespoon vegetable oil
1 medium-sized vegetable marrow, peeled, seeds removed and diced	1 medium-sized vegetable marrow, peeled, seeds removed and diced
6 spring onions, trimmed and finely chopped	6 spring onions, trimmed and finely chopped
1 × 15 ml spoon fresh tarragon, chopped or 1 × 5 ml spoon dried tarragon	1 tablespoon fresh tarragon, chopped or 1 teaspoon dried tarragon
Salt and freshly ground black pepper	Salt and freshly ground black pepper

Melt the butter with the oil in a saucepan. Add the diced marrow and finely chopped onions. Sauté for 3 minutes, turning frequently, until the juices begin to run from the marrow. Sprinkle in the tarragon and season to taste. Reduce the heat, cover and cook for 5 minutes, shaking the covered pan occasionally. Test one of the marrow dice with a skewer and if tender serve immediately in a warm vegetable dish. If not cooked, add 2 × 15 ml spoons / 2 tablespoons water and replace the pan over moderate heat until the marrow is tender.

Glazed carrots and parsnips

Here is a new way to combine two of the most frequently used vegetables, carrots and parsnips. Turnips may also be used for this dish.

Metric	Imperial
50 g butter	2 oz butter
4 large carrots, peeled and cut into rings	4 large carrots, peeled and cut into rings
2 large parsnips or turnips, peeled and cut into rings	2 large parsnips or turnips, peeled or cut into rings
1 × 2.5 ml spoon ground ginger	½ teaspoon ground ginger
1 × 2.5 ml spoon grated nutmeg	½ teaspoon grated nutmeg
Salt and freshly ground black pepper	Salt and freshly ground black pepper
2 × 15 ml spoons lemon juice	2 tablespoons lemon juice
2 × 15 ml spoons soft brown sugar	2 tablespoons soft brown sugar

Melt half the butter in a heavy saucepan and use to sauté the sliced carrots and parsnips gently, turning frequently, for 2 minutes. Add the ground ginger, grated nutmeg and seasoning to taste. Stir well, add the lemon juice and just sufficient water to cover the vegetables. Put on the lid and simmer, covered, for 12 to 15 minutes or until the vegetables are just tender and most of the liquid absorbed. Add the soft brown sugar and remaining butter and increase the heat slightly. Toss the vegetables frequently in the pan to glaze them evenly. Taste and adjust the seasoning if necessary. Serve as a snack with fried bacon or fried liver.

Glazed carrots and parsnips

Rembrandt's red cabbage

A Dutchman of this name, who does not claim the famous painter as his ancestor, invented this salad. It is very popular in Amsterdam, where it is more usual to include cardamom seeds than caraway seeds.

Metric	Imperial
¾ kg red cabbage	1½ lb red cabbage
4 red-skinned dessert apples	4 red-skinned dessert apples
50 g butter	2 oz butter
50 g currants	2 oz currants
4 × 15 ml spoons demerara sugar	4 tablespoons demerara sugar
4 × 15 ml spoons vinegar	4 tablespoons vinegar
2 × 15 ml spoons lemon juice	2 tablespoons lemon juice
150 ml water	¼ pint water
Salt and freshly ground black pepper	Salt and freshly ground black pepper
1 × 5 ml spoon caraway seeds	1 teaspoon caraway seeds

Remove outer leaves and core of the cabbage. Shred the remaining cabbage, put in a basin and pour boiling water over it. Allow to stand for 10 minutes. Core the apples, but do not peel them. Dice the apples. Drain the cabbage well.

Heat the butter in a large saucepan, add the cabbage and toss in the melted butter until well coated, over a moderate heat. Stir in the chopped apple and all the remaining ingredients, including the water. Cover, and cook over a low heat for 20 minutes, stirring from time to time. Taste and adjust the seasoning if necessary. Serve with boiled bacon, crisp fried bacon, or roast pork.

Rembrandt's red cabbage

Hot new potato salad

This unusual hot salad is inexpensive when home-grown new potatoes are in good supply. It should not be necessary to peel the cooked potatoes as so much of the nutritional value would be lost, but if you prefer, they are easier to peel when cooked and still warm.

Metric	Imperial
½ kg new potatoes, scrubbed	1 lb new potatoes, scrubbed
1 chicken stock cube	1 chicken stock cube
150 ml boiling water	¼ pint boiling water
¼ kg frozen peas	½ lb frozen peas
4 × 15 ml spoons mayonnaise	4 tablespoons mayonnaise
2 × 15 ml spoons chopped parsley and dill	2 tablespoons chopped parsley and dill
50 g gherkins, finely sliced, to garnish	2 oz gherkins, finely sliced, to garnish

Place the potatoes in a saucepan, cover with lightly salted water and bring to the boil. Cover and simmer until tender. Drain well and halve any larger potatoes while still warm. Transfer to a salad bowl.

Meanwhile, crumble the stock cube into the boiling water and stir until dissolved. Rinse out the saucepan in which the potatoes were cooked, pour in the stock, add the frozen peas and bring to the boil, stirring gently to separate the peas. Remove from the heat and transfer the peas from the stock to the potatoes with a slotted draining spoon.

Allow the stock to cool slightly then beat in the mayonnaise and stir in the chopped herbs. Pour this mixture over the potatoes and peas and fold over several times to coat the vegetables evenly with the dressing. Serve warm garnished with the sliced gherkin.

Hot new potato salad

Chinese leaf salad

Formerly considered an exotic oriental import, this crisp, crunchy leafed salad vegetable is now a popular alternative to hothouse lettuce when the latter is high in price.

Metric	Imperial
½ head Chinese leaves, washed	½ head Chinese leaves, washed
¼ kg cooked broad beans	½ lb cooked broad beans
2 × 15 ml spoons mustard sauce from jar of piccalilly	2 tablespoons mustard sauce from jar of piccalilly
4 × 15 ml spoons mayonnaise	4 tablespoons mayonnaise
FOR THE GARLIC CROÛTONS:	FOR THE GARLIC CROÛTONS:
2 × 15 ml spoons vegetable oil	2 tablespoons vegetable oil
1 clove of garlic, very finely chopped	1 clove of garlic, very finely chopped
2 slices white bread, trimmed and cut into dice	2 slices white bread, trimmed and cut into dice

Reserve one large outer leaf from the Chinese leaves for serving and shred the remainder finely. Place the shredded vegetable in a bowl with the broad beans.

Mix together the mustard sauce and the mayonnaise, pour over the leaves and beans and toss lightly. Allow to stand while preparing the garlic croûtons.

Heat the oil in a frying pan. Add the garlic and stir well. Drop in the bread cubes and fry them, stirring frequently, until crisp and golden-brown. Drain well.

Spoon the salad on to the reserved leaf on a serving dish and scatter over the garlic croûtons.

Chinese leaf salad

French bean and mushroom salad; Mushroom macédoine salad

French bean and mushroom salad

Raw mushrooms, when marinated in a dressing, are delicious. They lose no bulk, as when cooked, and combine well with French beans which often produce a glut during the summer.

Metric	Imperial
3 × 15 ml spoons vegetable oil	3 tablespoons vegetable oil
2 × 15 ml spoons lemon juice	2 tablespoons lemon juice
1 × 15 ml spoon chopped fresh mint	1 tablespoon chopped fresh mint
Salt and freshly ground black pepper	Salt and freshly ground black pepper
225 g button mushrooms, wiped and thinly sliced	½ lb button mushrooms, wiped and thinly sliced
½ kg young French beans, trimmed	1 lb young French beans, trimmed
TO FINISH:	TO FINISH:
Lettuce leaves	Lettuce leaves
2 × 5 ml spoons snipped chives	2 teaspoons snipped chives

To make the dressing, mix together the oil, lemon juice and chopped mint and seasoning to taste.

Place the mushrooms in a small bowl, pour over the dressing, cover and allow to marinate for several hours, or overnight if time permits.

Cook the beans, whole, in boiling lightly salted water for about 4 minutes, or until just tender but still slightly crisp. Drain and cool.

Combine the beans with the mushrooms and stir lightly with a fork to coat the beans with the dressing. Serve on a bed of lettuce leaves in a salad dish and scatter over the snipped chives.

Mushroom macédoine salad

A combination of mushrooms with frozen vegetables provides an interesting salad at any time of the year. This is a dish which could equally well be served hot or cold. Serve with fish and boiled potatoes for a light supper dish.

Metric	Imperial
¼ kg button mushrooms	½ lb button mushrooms
3 × 15 ml spoons vegetable oil	3 tablespoons vegetable oil
4 × 15 ml spoons salad cream	4 tablespoons salad cream
2 × 15 ml spoons single cream	2 tablespoons single cream
350 g frozen mixed vegetables, cooked	¾ lb frozen mixed vegetables, cooked
1 × 5 ml spoon finely chopped onion	1 teaspoon finely chopped onion
Salt and freshly ground black pepper	Salt and freshly ground black pepper
Watercress sprigs to garnish	Watercress sprigs to garnish

Wipe the mushrooms, but do not peel. Trim off the stalks level with the caps. Slice the mushrooms. Heat the oil in a frying pan and use to sauté the mushroom stalks and sliced caps for 2 minutes, until pale golden. Drain and cool on absorbent kitchen paper.

Stir together the salad cream and single cream in a large basin. Add the cooked mixed vegetables, chopped onion and mushrooms. Season, stir well, turn into a salad bowl and serve chilled, garnished with watercress sprigs.

NOTE: To serve hot, cook the mushrooms in a saucepan, add the other ingredients and heat through gently.

Gingered cucumber strips

An inexpensive salad when cucumbers are low in price, and particularly good with cold ham or roast pork.

Metric	Imperial
1 large cucumber, peeled	*1 large cucumber, peeled*
1 × 5 ml spoon salt	*1 teaspoon salt*
1 × 15 ml spoon finely chopped preserved ginger	*1 tablespoon finely chopped preserved ginger*
1 × 15 ml spoon ginger syrup from the jar	*1 tablespoon ginger syrup from the jar*
4 × 15 ml spoons white vinegar	*4 tablespoons white vinegar*

Cut the cucumber into finger lengths and then cut each length into 6 or 8 long thin strips, like large match sticks. Spread the strips out on a flat dish and sprinkle with the salt. Allow to stand for 30 minutes, then drain off the liquid and transfer to a bowl.

Mix the chopped ginger with the syrup and vinegar. Pour over the cucumber strips and toss together lightly. Serve the salad in a glass dish.

Gingered cucumber strips
Courgette and anchovy salad

Courgette and anchovy salad

There is now a comparatively long season when home-grown courgettes are cheap and plentiful. Although well-known as a hot vegetable they are less popular in salads. When cooking courgettes, it is worth preparing double the quantity and reserving some for this salad.

Metric	Imperial
1 × 15 ml spoon vegetable oil	*1 tablespoon vegetable oil*
½ kg courgettes, trimmed and thinly sliced	*1 lb courgettes, trimmed and thinly sliced*
6 spring onions, trimmed and chopped	*6 spring onions, trimmed and chopped*
150 ml chicken stock	*¼ pint chicken stock*
1 × 50 g can anchovy fillet	*1 × 2 oz can anchovy fillets*
2 × 15 ml spoons white vinegar	*2 tablespoons white vinegar*
1 × 5 ml spoon caster sugar	*1 teaspoon caster sugar*
Freshly ground black pepper	*Freshly ground black pepper*
1 clove of garlic, crushed	*1 clove of garlic, crushed*

Heat the oil in a saucepan. Add the sliced courgettes and spring onions and sauté over moderate heat until the vegetables are limp. Add the stock, cover and simmer for 5 minutes. Remove from the heat, stir well, cover again and allow to cool.

Remove the anchovies from the can, place on a board, and chop finely. Mix the vinegar, caster sugar, black pepper to taste and crushed garlic with the anchovy oil from the can. Stir in the chopped anchovies. Drain the cooked courgettes, toss them lightly in the dressing and serve in a glass dish. (No salt should be added to the cooking water for the courgettes or the basic dressing, as the anchovies are sufficiently salty.)

Chicory and grapefruit salad

Chicory and grapefruit salad

A rather unusual combination of flavours gives a fresh fruity tang to a winter green salad.

Metric
1 large ripe grapefruit
4 large heads chicory,
  trimmed and separated
  into leaves
FOR THE DRESSING:
150 ml soured cream
1 × 2.5 ml spoon French
  mustard
1 × 2.5 ml spoon salt
Good pinch of freshly
  ground black pepper
1 × 15 ml spoon white
  vinegar
1 × 15 ml spoon vegetable
  oil
1 × 5 ml spoon clear honey

Imperial
1 large ripe grapefruit
4 large heads chicory,
  trimmed and separated
  into leaves
FOR THE DRESSING:
¼ pint soured cream
½ teaspoon French
  mustard
½ teaspoon salt
Good pinch of freshly
  ground black pepper
1 tablespoon white vinegar
1 tablespoon vegetable oil
1 teaspoon clear honey

TO GARNISH:
1 × 15 ml spoon chopped
  parsley

TO GARNISH:
1 tablespoon chopped
  parsley

Grate a little zest from the skin of the grapefruit. (As it is strongly flavoured, add it gradually to the finished dressing, tasting to make sure the flavour does not become too strong.) Peel the grapefruit, remove all white pith, separate into segments, and cut each of these in half. Place in a bowl. Reserve about 16 well-shaped leaves of chicory to line a salad bowl and chop the rest roughly and add to the grapefruit. Place the reserved chicory leaves in a polythene bag to keep them fresh.

To make the dressing, put the soured cream in a small basin and beat in the mustard, salt, pepper, vinegar and oil. Stir in the honey. Add sufficient grated zest to give a hint of grapefruit to the flavour. Pour the dressing over the chopped grapefruit segments and chicory and toss lightly.

Arrange the chicory leaves to make a decorative border on a round platter and pile up the salad in the centre. Scatter the chopped parsley over the salad to garnish.

80

Carrot, apple and nut salad

A colourful salad – creamy-white speckled with orange, green and scarlet – this makes a good contrast with the conventional green salad.

Metric

1 × 15 ml spoon lemon juice
1 red-skinned dessert apple, cored and thinly sliced
2 large carrots, peeled and grated
100 g white cabbage, core removed and finely shredded
1 leek, white and pale green part only, washed and finely sliced
8 walnut halves

FOR THE DRESSING:
1 × 15 ml spoon lemon juice
1 × 2.5 ml spoon caster sugar
1 × 2.5 ml spoon salt
Pinch of freshly ground black pepper
2 × 15 ml spoons vegetable oil
1 × 15 ml spoon smooth peanut butter

Imperial

1 tablespoon lemon juice
1 red-skinned dessert apple, cored and thinly sliced
2 large carrots, peeled and grated
¼ lb white cabbage, core removed and finely shredded
1 leek, white and pale green part only, washed and finely sliced
8 walnut halves

FOR THE DRESSING:
1 tablespoon lemon juice
½ teaspoon caster sugar
½ teaspoon salt
Pinch of freshly ground black pepper
2 tablespoons vegetable oil
1 tablespoon smooth peanut butter

Pour the lemon juice into a saucer. Dip the apple slices in the lemon juice and coat both sides to prevent discoloration. Arrange the grated carrot, shredded cabbage, sliced leek and apple slices in a salad bowl. Scatter the walnut halves over the top.

To make the dressing, place the lemon juice, sugar, salt and pepper in a small basin and beat vigorously until blended. Gradually beat in the oil and peanut butter alternately, until the dressing is smooth and slightly thickened. To save time, place all the ingredients in a screw-topped jar and shake briskly until the dressing emulsifies. Pour the dressing over the salad and toss lightly before serving.

Carrot, apple and nut salad

Mix all the ingredients for the dressing except the oil, and gradually beat in the oil so that it emulsifies and thickens the dressing. Allow to stand for at least 1 hour.

Chop the raisins and walnuts roughly. Grate the carrot. Remove coarse strings from the celery and chop. Remove seeds, core and white pith from the green pepper and cut into thin strips. Separate the endive heads into the leaves. Toss all the salad ingredients lightly in the dressing, and serve chilled with assorted cold meats, or with hot roast beef or pork.

Melon in curry cream

Although melon is usually thought of as a sweet fruit unsuitable for salad use, it is quite delicious combined with this delicately spiced creamy dressing, and especially good served with cold ham.

Metric	Imperial
1 medium-sized melon, preferably honeydew, peeled and quartered	1 medium-sized melon, preferably honeydew, peeled and quartered
FOR THE CURRY CREAM:	FOR THE CURRY CREAM:
50 g butter	2 oz butter
1 small onion, peeled and finely chopped	1 small onion, peeled and finely chopped
2 inner stalks celery, scrubbed and chopped	2 inner stalks celery, scrubbed and chopped
3 × 15 ml spoons flour	3 tablespoons flour
1 × 15 ml spoon curry powder	1 tablespoon curry powder
1 × 5 ml spoon soft brown sugar	1 teaspoon soft brown sugar
1 × 2.5 ml spoon ground bay leaves	½ teaspoon ground bay leaves
3 × 15 ml spoons lemon juice	3 tablespoons lemon juice
150 ml milk	¼ pint milk
150 ml chicken stock	¼ pint chicken stock
4 × 15 ml spoons single cream	4 tablespoons single cream
Salt	Salt
Pinch of curry powder to garnish (optional)	Pinch of curry powder to garnish (optional)

Place the melon quarters on a large dish and carefully remove the seeds, reserving the juice. Discard the seeds. Dice the melon flesh neatly, and place in a glass serving dish.

To make the curry cream, melt the butter in a saucepan with a heavy base. Add the chopped onion and celery and cook gently until limp. Stir in the flour and curry powder and cook over low heat for 2 minutes, stirring all the time. Add the sugar, ground bay leaves, lemon juice, reserved melon juice, milk and stock and bring to the boil, stirring constantly. Lower the heat, cover and simmer for 15 minutes. Cool, stir in the cream and add salt to taste. Chill well.

Pour the curry cream over the melon dice and, if liked, garnish with a pinch of curry powder. Serve very cold.

Sweet winter salad; Melon in curry cream

Sweet winter salad

Metric	Imperial
100 g seedless raisins	¼ lb seedless raisins
50 g shelled walnuts	2 oz shelled walnuts
100 g carrots, peeled	¼ lb carrots, peeled
2 stalks celery, scrubbed	2 stalks celery, scrubbed
1 sweet green pepper	1 sweet green pepper
2 small heads endive, trimmed	2 small heads endive, trimmed
FOR THE DRESSING:	FOR THE DRESSING:
2 × 5 ml spoons lemon juice	2 teaspoons lemon juice
Salt and freshly ground black pepper	Salt and freshly ground black pepper
1 × 5 ml spoon clear honey	1 teaspoon clear honey
3 × 15 ml spoons salad oil	3 tablespoons salad oil

Rosy coleslaw; Piquant yogurt dressing; Wine vinaigrette

Rosy coleslaw

This makes a delightful alternative to the usual creamy-white coleslaw. It is pink, and has a lightly fruited flavour, which can be enhanced by folding in a small quantity of diced beetroot.

Metric	Imperial
3–4 × 15 ml spoons cranberry sauce	3–4 tablespoons cranberry sauce
4 × 15 ml spoons mayonnaise	4 tablespoons mayonnaise
1 × 15 ml spoon white vinegar	1 tablespoon white vinegar
Salt and freshly ground black pepper	Salt and freshly ground black pepper
½ kg white cabbage, core removed and finely shredded	1 lb white cabbage, core removed and finely shredded
Chopped chives to garnish	Chopped chives to garnish

Combine the cranberry sauce, mayonnaise and vinegar in a bowl and season to taste.

Add the shredded cabbage gradually, tossing it to coat well with the dressing. Cover and chill for at least 2 hours.

Spoon the coleslaw into a glass salad bowl and serve sprinkled with chopped chives.

Two useful salad dressings

Here are two dressings either of which will lift a simple green salad out of the ordinary. The yogurt dressing is creamy without being as rich or expensive to make as mayonnaise. These dressings will keep for up to three days in screw-topped jars in the refrigerator. Shake well each time before serving.

Piquant yogurt dressing
Beat together 1 × 15 ml spoon / 1 tablespoon each corn oil, lemon juice and drained capers. Stir in 150 ml / ¼ pint unsweetened natural yogurt and season to taste with salt and freshly ground black pepper.

Wine vinaigrette
Whisk together 1 × 5 ml spoon / 1 teaspoon French mustard and 1 × 15 ml spoon / 1 tablespoon wine vinegar. Season to taste with salt and freshly ground black pepper. Gradually add 4 × 15 ml spoons / 4 tablespoons each dry white wine and corn oil, whisking all the time to emulsify the oil. Stir in 1 × 15 ml spoon / 1 tablespoon each chopped spring onion and parsley.

Family fillers - snacks and sandwiches

At tea time, or whatever time of the day some hungry member of the family requires a snack, these are substantial enough to make a light meal. Each recipe is chosen for a special reason; either because it can be quickly prepared from food in the store cupboard, or because it makes use of the reasonably priced fillers such as minced beef and sausages. If you own a freezer, it would be an advantage to make up a few of these recipes, choosing those which will quickly defrost and reheat in the oven at very short notice.

For those who are happy with sandwiches as a snack, there is a tasty fish spread suitable for fresh buttered bread or crispbreads. Then there are more elaborate ideas for hot sandwiches, toasted and finished under the grill or fried in a little oil – very little is needed if you use a non-stick frying pan

Potted hough or shin of beef; Beefeater pie; Minced beef and bacon roll

Potted hough or shin of beef

It is necessary to use the particular cut of beef suggested in this recipe as its gelatinous nature ensures a good set. Try to make this dish when the oven is already being used for another requiring long, slow cooking.

Metric	Imperial
½ kg hough or shin of beef	1 lb hough or shin of beef
2 rashers streaky bacon	2 rashers streaky bacon
1 carrot, peeled	1 carrot, peeled
1 onion, peeled and stuck with a few cloves	1 onion, peeled and stuck with a few cloves
450 ml water	¾ pint water
1 × 2.5 ml spoon salt	½ teaspoon salt
Freshly ground black pepper	Freshly ground black pepper

Cut the beef into very small pieces. Put into a flameproof casserole with the bacon, carrot and onion. Add the water and bring to the boil. Remove any scum with a slotted draining spoon, season to taste and cover with a close-fitting lid. Cook in a cool oven (150°C/300°F or Gas Mark 2) for 3 hours.

Remove the vegetables and the rind from the bacon, and discard. Chop the beef and bacon finely. Put the meat into a 1 litre/1¾ pint basin or mould. Strain over sufficient stock to cover and put in a cool place. When cold cover with foil and chill in a refrigerator overnight until set.

This jellied meat mould is delicious served sliced in sandwiches or with potatoes and a green salad.

Beefeater pie

The toasted sandwich triangles add a most attractive finish to this unusual supper dish.

Metric	Imperial
50 g dripping	2 oz dripping
1 large onion, peeled and finely chopped	1 large onion, peeled and finely chopped
1 clove of garlic, crushed	1 clove of garlic, crushed
¼ kg minced beef	½ lb minced beef
2 × 15 ml spoons tomato purée	2 tablespoons tomato purée
300 ml beef stock	½ pint beef stock
3 × 15 ml spoons quick cook oats	3 tablespoons quick cook oats
Salt and freshly ground black pepper	Salt and freshly ground black pepper
4 slices white bread	4 slices white bread
1 × 75 g jar chicken and bacon spread	1 × 3 oz jar chicken and bacon spread
2 tomatoes, sliced	2 tomatoes, sliced
Chopped parsley to garnish	Chopped parsley to garnish

Melt the dripping in a saucepan, add the chopped onion and crushed garlic and fry gently until limp. Add the minced beef and fry until crumbly, stirring occasionally. Stir in the tomato purée and the stock, and sprinkle in the oats. Continue stirring until the mixture comes to the boil, then season to taste. Reduce the heat, cover and simmer for 30 minutes, stirring frequently.

Five minutes before the beef mixture is cooked, remove the crusts from the bread and spread each slice with the chicken and bacon spread. Sandwich 2 slices, spread side inside, together. Toast both sides of the sandwiches lightly and then cut each one into 4 triangles. Spoon the beef mixture into a flameproof dish and arrange the tomato slices on top. Place under a hot grill for a minute or two to heat the tomato slices, then arrange the sandwich triangles around the edge of the dish and sprinkle with chopped parsley.

Minced beef and bacon roll

This meat roll can be served hot with plenty of gravy and vegetables. It is also excellent cold and can be sliced thinly to make delicious sandwiches.

Metric	Imperial
½ kg minced beef	1 lb minced beef
¼ kg minced bacon (trimmings may be used)	½ lb minced bacon (trimmings may be used)
225 g fresh white breadcrumbs	½ lb fresh white breadcrumbs
1 medium-sized onion, peeled and finely chopped	1 medium-sized onion, peeled and finely chopped
1 × 5 ml spoon chopped parsley	1 teaspoon chopped parsley
Pinch of dried thyme	Pinch of dried thyme
Pinch of dried marjoram	Pinch of dried marjoram
Salt and freshly ground black pepper	Salt and freshly ground black pepper
2 eggs, lightly beaten	2 eggs, lightly beaten

Put the minced beef and bacon into a bowl and break up with a fork. Add the breadcrumbs, chopped onion, herbs and seasoning and blend well together. Bind the mixture with the beaten eggs and shape into a roll.

Wrap the roll in greased aluminium foil, sealing carefully by folding and crimping the edges of the foil.

Place in a steamer over gently bubbling water and cook for 2 hours, taking care that the pan does not boil dry. Replenish the pan with more boiling water if necessary. Remove from the foil and serve hot immediately. If serving cold, allow the roll to cool in the foil.

NOTE: The prepared mixture may be divided and shaped to make 2 smaller rolls, one for serving hot and one cold.

Corned beef cheeseburger

Corned beef cheeseburgers

These burgers are easy to make and good to eat.

Metric	Imperial
350 g lean cut corned beef	¾ lb lean cut corned beef
1 medium-sized onion, peeled	1 medium-sized onion, peeled
1 egg	1 egg
1 × 15 ml spoon Worcestershire sauce	1 tablespoon Worcestershire sauce
50 g quick cook oats	2 oz quick cook oats
1 × 15 ml spoon chopped parsley	1 tablespoon chopped parsley
Salt and freshly ground black pepper	Salt and freshly ground black pepper
Vegetable oil for frying	Vegetable oil for frying
4 slices processed cheese	4 slices processed cheese
1 tomato	1 tomato

Place the corned beef in a medium-sized bowl and mash it with a fork until completely broken down. Grate the onion straight into the corned beef. Beat the egg and add to the meat mixture with the Worcestershire sauce, oats, parsley and seasoning to taste. Mix together thoroughly and allow the mixture to stand for 5 minutes. Divide into 4 equal parts and shape each into a round approx. 2.5 cm/1 inch thick.

Heat a little oil in a frying pan and cook the burgers for 2 to 3 minutes on each side, until golden-brown. Remove from the pan and drain well on absorbent kitchen paper.

Meanwhile, heat the grill. Place the burgers in the grill pan and top with a slice of cheese. Place under the grill until the cheese melts. Top with tomato slices. Serve with baps (see page 111) and sweet pickles.

Sausage, egg and bacon pie

A savoury plate pie which makes a tasty, easy-to-eat snack supper. If you have a freezer it is a good standby dish for unexpected visitors.

Metric	Imperial
350 g puff pastry	¾ lb puff pastry
¼ kg beef sausages, cooked and chopped	½ lb beef sausages, cooked and chopped
4 hard-boiled eggs, shelled and chopped	4 hard-boiled eggs, shelled and chopped
175 g lean bacon, chopped	6 oz lean bacon, chopped
1 onion, peeled and grated	1 onion, peeled and grated
Salt and freshly ground black pepper	Salt and freshly ground black pepper
1 egg, beaten, to glaze	1 egg, beaten, to glaze
1 tomato, sliced	1 tomato, sliced
150 ml soured cream	¼ pint soured cream

Divide the pastry into 2 equal portions, and roll each one to a circle about 22.5 cm/9 inches in diameter. Line a shallow pie plate with one circle of pastry. Mix the chopped, cooked sausages with the chopped hard-boiled egg, chopped bacon, grated onion and seasoning. Spoon evenly on to the pastry-lined plate, leaving a 2.5 cm/1 inch rim around the edge. Brush the pastry rim with beaten egg. Cover the filling with the remaining circle of pastry, and trim off any excess. Pinch the pastry edges together to seal. Brush the top of the pastry with beaten egg and make a small steam vent in the centre of the pie.

Bake in a fairly hot oven (200°C/400°F or Gas Mark 6) for 40 minutes. Arrange tomato slices on top of the pie for the last 5 minutes of cooking time. Remove from the oven and carefully make the hole in the top of the pie crust slightly larger. Stir the soured cream to thin it and carefully pour it through a small funnel into the pie. Leave for a few minutes before serving.

Serves 6

Sausage, egg and bacon pie

Meanwhile, mix together the oats, self-raising flour, half the Parmesan cheese, the salt and the mixed herbs in a bowl. Rub in the margarine until the mixture resembles coarse breadcrumbs. Add sufficient milk to make a fairly stiff dough.

Divide the mixture into 2 equal portions and roll each out on a floured board to a circle approx. 20 cm/8 inches in diameter. Place one half in the bottom of a well-greased 20 cm/8 inch ovenproof dish. Pile the cold sausage mixture on top and cover with the remaining round of dough, pressing the edges together well down into the dish. Brush the top with milk and sprinkle the remaining Parmesan cheese on top. Bake in a fairly hot oven (190°C/375°F or Gas Mark 5) for 30 to 35 minutes.

Sausages with horseradish mayonnaise

Sausages are an unusual ingredient to find in a salad. This special 'winter' salad can either be served on its own, or as a topping for open sandwiches.

Metric	Imperial
½ kg pork sausages	1 lb pork sausages
4 × 15 ml spoons French dressing	4 tablespoons French dressing
FOR THE HORSERADISH MAYONNAISE:	FOR THE HORSERADISH MAYONNAISE:
2 egg yolks	2 egg yolks
1 × 15 ml spoon wine vinegar	1 tablespoon wine vinegar
2 × 5 ml spoons French mustard	2 teaspoons French mustard
300 ml olive oil	½ pint olive oil
Salt and freshly ground black pepper	Salt and freshly ground black pepper
4 × 15 ml spoons whipped cream	4 tablespoons whipped cream
1 × 15 ml spoon creamed horseradish	1 tablespoon creamed horseradish
2 stalks of celery, scrubbed and chopped	2 stalks of celery, scrubbed and chopped
2 eating apples, diced	2 eating apples, diced
2 × 15 ml spoons diced gherkin	2 tablespoons diced gherkin

Grill the pork sausages for about 10 minutes, until golden-brown all over and cooked through. While they are still warm put them into a shallow dish and spoon over the French dressing. Cover the dish and chill in the refrigerator for 2 hours.

To make the horseradish mayonnaise, beat the egg yolks with the wine vinegar and then add the French mustard. Gradually add the oil, in a fine trickle, whisking continuously until it is all absorbed. Season to taste and stir in the whipped cream and creamed horseradish. Fold in the chopped celery, grated apple and chopped gherkin.

Arrange the marinated sausages on a serving platter and spoon over the horseradish mayonnaise. Serve with rye bread.

Savoury shortcake; Sausages with horseradish mayonnaise

Savoury shortcake

An unusual shortcake to serve hot or cold, with a nutty savoury taste.

Metric	Imperial
100 g bacon pieces or streaky bacon	¼ lb bacon pieces or streaky bacon
¼ kg skinless pork sausages, thinly sliced	½ lb skinless pork sausages, thinly sliced
100 g button mushrooms, wiped and sliced	¼ lb button mushrooms, wiped and sliced
100 g quick cook oats	¼ lb quick cook oats
100 g self-raising flour	¼ lb self-raising flour
50 g grated Parmesan cheese	2 oz grated Parmesan cheese
Pinch of salt	Pinch of salt
1 × 5 ml spoon mixed dried herbs	1 teaspoon mixed dried herbs
100 g margarine	¼ lb margarine
Approx. 150 ml milk to bind and glaze	Approx. ¼ pint milk to bind and glaze

Derind the bacon and cut into very small pieces. Place the bacon in a frying pan and fry gently until the fat begins to run. Stir in the sliced sausages and mushrooms. Allow the mixture to become quite cold.

Cod's roe spread

This spread is delicious as a filling for sandwiches. For a buffet party, decorate with strips of anchovy, slices of stuffed green olives and lemon slices.

Metric	Imperial
1 kg fresh cod's roe	2 lb fresh cod's roe
4 peppercorns	4 peppercorns
1 bay leaf	1 bay leaf
1 blade of mace	1 blade of mace
100 g butter	¼ lb butter
1 × 5 ml spoon tarragon vinegar	1 teaspoon tarragon vinegar
1 × 5 ml spoon lemon juice	1 teaspoon lemon juice
1 × 2.5 ml spoon anchovy essence	½ teaspoon anchovy essence
Salt and freshly ground black pepper	Salt and freshly ground black pepper

Wash the roes well, tie them in muslin and place in a saucepan with the peppercorns, bay leaf and mace. Cover with boiling water. Bring back to the boil, cover and simmer for 20 minutes. Take the roe from the pan. Discard the muslin and the skin from the roe.

Put the roe into a basin and mash with a fork. Beat in the butter, vinegar, lemon juice and anchovy essence. Taste and add seasoning if necessary. Beat well until smooth or use an electric blender to make a smooth paste. Press into a buttered mould. Cover with a weighted plate and allow to cool. Refrigerate until required.

NOTE: Tinned cod's roe may be used if fresh is unavailable.

Cod's roe spread

Savoury mushroom toasts; Kipper goujons with soured cream sauce

Kipper goujons with soured cream sauce

These strips of kipper fillets covered with a crisp cheesy coating team up well with this sharp cream sauce. Serve with toast as a supper dish or inexpensive first course for a special occasion.

Metric	Imperial
FOR THE SAUCE:	FOR THE SAUCE:
150 ml soured cream	¼ pint soured cream
1 × 15 ml spoon lemon juice	1 tablespoon lemon juice
1 × 5 ml spoon chopped drained capers	1 teaspoon chopped drained capers
1 × 15 ml spoon milk	1 tablespoon milk
1 × 5 ml spoon chopped parsley	1 teaspoon chopped parsley
Good pinch of cayenne pepper	Good pinch of cayenne pepper
Salt and freshly ground black pepper	Salt and freshly ground black pepper
FOR THE GOUJONS:	FOR THE GOUJONS:
1 × 275 g packet kipper fillets	1 × 10 oz packet kipper fillets
100 g quick cook oats	¼ lb quick cook oats
25 g grated Parmesan cheese	1 oz grated Parmesan cheese
1 egg, beaten	1 egg, beaten
1 × 15 ml spoon milk	1 tablespoon milk
Vegetable oil for frying	Vegetable oil for frying

To make the sauce, place the soured cream, lemon juice, capers, milk, parsley and seasonings in a bowl and mix thoroughly. Chill in the refrigerator until required.

Fried silverside sandwiches

An excellent alternative to corned beef hash is a fried beef sandwich, dipped in beaten egg to make it even more nourishing.

Metric	Imperial
25 g butter	1 oz butter
8 large slices white bread	8 large slices white bread
4 × 15 ml spoons sweet brown pickles	4 tablespoons sweet brown pickles
4 slices beef silverside	4 slices beef silverside
2 eggs, beaten	2 eggs, beaten
75 ml milk	3 fl oz milk
Freshly ground black pepper	Freshly ground black pepper
Vegetable oil for frying	Vegetable oil for frying
Mustard and cress to garnish	Mustard and cress to garnish

Thinly butter the slices of bread and spread with the pickles. Lay the slices of beef silverside on 4 of the bread slices and cover with the remaining slices, so that the pickle helps the bread to adhere to the meat. Place the sandwiches on a board, press firmly together and cut each one across diagonally to make 2 triangles.

Beat up the eggs with the milk, season with a little black pepper and pour into a shallow dish. Dip the sandwiches in the egg mixture, using food tongs to turn them. Make sure they are completely coated.

Heat a little oil in a frying pan and quickly fry the triangles on both sides until golden-brown. Serve hot garnished with mustard and cress.

Fried silverside sandwiches

Remove the skin from the kipper fillets and cut each fillet into equal strips. Mix together the oats and the Parmesan cheese. Beat the egg with the milk. Dip the kipper strips first in the beaten egg and then in the oat mixture, pressing firmly to ensure the goujons are well coated. Heat the oil in a deep-fat fryer or saucepan until it is hot enough to turn a stale bread cube golden-brown in 45 seconds (185°C/360°F). Fry the kipper goujons for about 2 minutes, until golden-brown. Drain well, on absorbent kitchen paper, pile up in a serving dish and serve with soured cream sauce.

Savoury mushroom toasts

When a hot snack is required rather than a sandwich, it is usually required in a hurry. These toast treats take only a few minutes to prepare.

Metric	Imperial
40 g butter	1½ oz butter
100 g button mushrooms, wiped and thinly sliced	¼ lb button mushrooms, wiped and thinly sliced
4 large slices white bread	4 large slices white bread
1 × 75 g jar chicken and bacon spread	1 × 3 oz jar chicken and bacon spread
2 × 5 ml spoons chopped parsley to garnish	2 teaspoons chopped parsley to garnish

Melt 15 g / ½ oz of the butter in a small frying pan and use to fry the sliced mushrooms until golden. Meanwhile, toast the bread lightly and spread one side of each slice with the remaining butter. Spread the buttered toast fairly thickly with the chicken and bacon spread and arrange the cooked mushrooms on top.

Place the toasts under a hot grill for 2 minutes. Serve hot, scattered with chopped parsley and cut into fingers.

Pasta and rice dishes

The basic rules for cooking pasta perfectly are very important and are fully explained in this chapter. Now that the housewife is becoming more familiar with pasta cookery, the time has arrived to experiment far more widely than with simple spaghetti sauces. Egg tagliatelli is particularly nourishing and has a beautiful golden colour. Lasagne verde, coloured green with the addition of spinach, makes a beautiful contrast with any of the usual sauces for spaghetti and in the two recipes for lasagne, either white or green pasta could be used. Really unusual ways to create main dishes with pasta as a base are suggested with both fish and meat, to show the versatility of this economical, all-purpose food.

Rice cookery is not merely a matter of boiling long- or round-grain rice until soft, or indeed to a mushy consistency which spoils the delicate but nutty flavour of rice. Various methods of cooking it are carefully explained here because this makes rice a much more versatile product. A risotto or pilaff is entirely different from any dish made with boiled rice and many people feel they are much more acceptable in texture and taste. Again, all sorts of other ingredients can be introduced to turn a basic rice mixture into a main dish.

Basic rules for pasta cookery

Pasta is by today's standards wonderfully cheap and filling for what it costs. It has taken its place among the staple items in the kitchen cupboard on which housewives build a cheap and nutritious diet. Fortunately it comes in a great variety of shapes and forms, all of which are quick and easy to cook. Here are the essential rules:

1. Cook pasta in a large saucepan in plenty of salted boiling water. The saucepan must be large enough to allow the contents to boil really fast during cooking without boiling over. Do not cover the pan. According to size, the pasta will take anything from 4 to 15 minutes to cook. When ready it should be 'al dente' or still reasonably firm when tested.

2. Drain the cooked pasta thoroughly. It is improved by rinsing immediately after draining with fresh hot water, both to prevent it from continuing to cook in its own heat, and to remove any excess starch.

3. If you are serving the pasta simply with a sauce, either return the drained pasta to the rinsed-out pan with a little melted butter in it to coat the strands, or turn it straight into the rinsed-out pan and stir in a little oil for the same purpose.

4. As a guide, 75 g/3 oz of uncooked pasta is sufficient per person for a light dish, and 100 g/¼ lb for a main dish.

Barbecued spaghetti

Spaghetti mixed with a hot spicy sauce to make a change from the more usual Italian style recipe.

Metric	Imperial
2 × 15 ml spoons vegetable oil	2 tablespoons vegetable oil
1 medium-sized onion, peeled and finely chopped	1 medium-sized onion, peeled and finely chopped
1–2 × 15 ml spoons curry powder	1–2 tablespoons curry powder
3 × 15 ml spoons peanut butter	3 tablespoons peanut butter
2 × 5 ml spoons tomato purée	2 teaspoons tomato purée
Small strip of lemon rind	Small strip of lemon rind
300 ml chicken stock	½ pint chicken stock
Salt and freshly ground black pepper	Salt and freshly ground black pepper
225–350 g spaghetti	½–¾ lb spaghetti

Heat the oil in a saucepan. Add the chopped onion and fry until just beginning to turn golden. Stir in the curry powder and fry for a few seconds. Add the peanut butter, tomato purée, lemon rind, stock and seasoning to taste. Bring to the boil, stirring constantly, cover and simmer for about 15 minutes, stirring occasionally. Remove the piece of lemon rind. Taste and add more seasoning if necessary.

Meanwhile, cook the spaghetti in plenty of boiling lightly salted water. Drain well. Add the spaghetti to the sauce and mix until well coated. Serve hot with grilled sausages or beefburgers.

Barbecued spaghetti

Sweet-sour pork and pasta

Sweet-sour pork and pasta

The Chinese have evolved many delicious sauces to serve with rice and with pasta. In this recipe, one of the best known sauces from China, sweet-sour, gives pasta a most unusual and appetizing flavour.

Metric	Imperial
½ kg pork shoulder steaks	1 lb pork shoulder steaks
Salt and freshly ground black pepper	Salt and freshly ground black pepper
4 × 15 ml spoons vinegar	4 tablespoons vinegar
2 × 15 ml spoons brown sugar	2 tablespoons brown sugar
2 × 15 ml spoons soya sauce	2 tablespoons soya sauce
50 g butter	2 oz butter
1 × 396 g can tomatoes	1 × 14 oz can tomatoes
1 × 15 ml spoon tomato purée	1 tablespoon tomato purée
Juice and grated zest of 1 large orange	Juice and grated zest of 1 large orange
350 g pasta shells	¾ lb pasta shells

Cut the pork into thin strips. Put into a shallow dish with seasoning, vinegar, brown sugar and soya sauce. Cover and chill in the refrigerator overnight. Remove the meat from the marinade and drain well. Heat the butter in a pan and fry the pork strips gently until browned on all sides. Add the marinade, canned tomatoes and their liquid, tomato purée and orange juice and zest. Cover and simmer for 30 to 35 minutes.

Meanwhile, cook the pasta in rapidly boiling salted water, for about 6 to 8 minutes, until just tender. Drain well. Pile up the cooked pasta on to a warm serving dish and spoon over the sweet-sour pork sauce.

Macaroni cheese balls with Spanish sauce

Small savoury balls with a crisp coating are deep-fried and served with a chunky, garlic-flavoured tomato sauce.

Metric	Imperial
¼ kg short-cut macaroni	½ lb short-cut macaroni
50 g butter	2 oz butter
50 g plain flour	2 oz plain flour
300 ml milk	½ pint milk
1 × 2.5 ml spoon salt	½ teaspoon salt
1 × 2.5 ml spoon dry mustard	½ teaspoon dry mustard
¼ kg cheese, grated	½ lb cheese, grated
2 eggs, beaten	2 eggs, beaten
Vegetable oil for frying	Vegetable oil for frying
FOR THE COATING:	FOR THE COATING:
2 eggs, beaten	2 eggs, beaten
175 g dry breadcrumbs	6 oz dry breadcrumbs
FOR THE SAUCE:	FOR THE SAUCE:
4 × 15 ml spoons vegetable oil	4 tablespoons vegetable oil
1 onion, peeled and finely chopped	1 onion, peeled and finely chopped
2 cloves of garlic, crushed	2 cloves of garlic, crushed
1 small green pepper, deseeded and chopped	1 small green pepper, deseeded and chopped
1 × 396 g can tomatoes	1 × 14 oz can tomatoes
1 × 5 ml spoon dried mixed herbs	1 teaspoon dried mixed herbs
Salt and freshly ground black pepper	Salt and freshly ground black pepper
2 × 5 ml spoons cornflour	2 teaspoons cornflour

Cook the macaroni in plenty of boiling lightly salted water. Drain well. Place the butter, flour, milk, salt and mustard together in a saucepan and whisk over moderate heat until the mixture comes to the boil. Cook for 2 minutes. Remove from the heat and add the cheese. Stir in the beaten eggs and the macaroni. Allow to become almost cold and then divide the mixture into 12 to 16 equal portions. With clean wet hands shape each portion into a ball and coat with the beaten eggs and then the breadcrumbs. The balls must be completely coated so repeat the process if necessary.

To make the sauce, heat the oil in a saucepan. Add the chopped onion and the crushed garlic and fry until the onion is soft but not browned. Add the chopped pepper, tomatoes and their liquid and the herbs. Season to taste. Moisten the cornflour with a little cold water and stir into the tomato mixture. Bring to the boil, stirring constantly, reduce the heat and simmer for 15 minutes.

To fry the macaroni cheese balls, heat the oil in a deep-fat fryer or saucepan until it is hot enough to turn a stale bread cube golden-brown in 45 seconds (185°C/360°F). Fry the balls, a few at a time, until golden-brown. Pile up on a warm serving dish and hand the sauce separately.

Macaroni cheese balls with Spanish sauce; Smoked cod jumble (right)

Smoked cod jumble

Children love this dish, especially piled up on thick slices of freshly made, buttered toast. If preferred, haddock may be used in place of cod.

Metric	Imperial
¼ kg macaroni	½ lb macaroni
75 g butter	3 oz butter
350 g smoked cod or haddock fillet, skinned and cut into chunks	¾ lb smoked cod or haddock fillet, skinned and cut into chunks
4 tomatoes, chopped	4 tomatoes, chopped
6 spring onions, trimmed and chopped	6 spring onions, trimmed and chopped
Salt and freshly ground black pepper	Salt and freshly ground black pepper

Cook the macaroni in plenty of boiling slightly salted water. Drain well. Melt the butter in a saucepan. Add the fish, cover and cook very gently for 10 minutes, or until the fish is tender. Remove the lid, add the cooked macaroni, chopped tomato and spring onion and season carefully. Stir the mixture lightly to avoid breaking up the fish, and reheat well. Serve with hot buttered toast.

Souffléed pasta bolognese

Souffléed pasta bolognese

Many different varieties of pasta can be teamed with a bolognese sauce – in this recipe the pasta and sauce are given a 'soufflé' texture by incorporating whisked egg whites.

Metric	Imperial
3 × 15 ml spoons vegetable oil	3 tablespoons vegetable oil
175 g pasta shapes	6 oz pasta shapes
1 large onion, peeled and finely chopped	1 large onion, peeled and finely chopped
¼ kg minced beef	½ lb minced beef
1 clove of garlic, crushed	1 clove of garlic, crushed
1 × 15 ml spoon tomato purée	1 tablespoon tomato purée
1 × 396 g can tomatoes	1 × 14 oz can tomatoes
Salt and freshly ground black pepper	Salt and freshly ground black pepper
3 eggs, separated	3 eggs, separated
25 g grated Parmesan cheese	1 oz grated Parmesan cheese

Bring a large pan of lightly salted water to the boil and add 1 × 15 ml spoon / 1 tablespoon of the oil. Add the pasta shapes and cook until just tender – about 6 minutes. Drain well.

Fry the chopped onion gently in the remaining oil for 5 minutes. Add the minced beef and continue frying gently until lightly browned. Stir in the crushed garlic, tomato purée, canned tomatoes and their liquid and seasoning to taste. Simmer for 20 minutes. Allow to cool and then beat the egg yolks into the bolognese sauce. Fold in the cooked pasta. Stiffly beat the egg whites and fold in. Put into a greased ovenproof dish and sprinkle the surface with grated Parmesan cheese. Bake in a fairly hot oven (190°C/375°F or Gas Mark 5) for 40 to 45 minutes until risen and golden-brown. Serve immediately with extra grated Parmesan cheese.
Serves 4 to 6

Lasagne ham rolls

Smoked haddock and egg lasagne

Lasagne ham rolls

This pasta dish is particularly quick and easy to prepare – once cooked, the rolls of lasagne resemble cannelloni, which is not quite so easily obtainable.

Metric	Imperial
1 × 15 ml spoon vegetable oil	1 tablespoon vegetable oil
175 g lasagne (about 8 sheets)	6 oz lasagne (about 8 sheets)
8 thin slices ham	8 thin slices ham
2 × 15 ml spoons French mustard	2 tablespoons French mustard
100 g Cheddar cheese, grated	¼ lb Cheddar cheese, grated
Salt and freshly ground black pepper	Salt and freshly ground black pepper
1 × 425 g can mushroom soup	1 × 15 oz can mushroom soup
2 large tomatoes, sliced	2 large tomatoes, sliced
Parsley sprigs to garnish	Parsley sprigs to garnish

Bring a large pan of lightly salted water to the boil and add the oil. Lower the sheets of lasagne, one at a time, into the pan and cook for 5 minutes. Drain well and lay the sheets of lasagne on a large piece of greased greaseproof paper or foil. Lay a slice of ham on top of each sheet of lasagne and spread with French mustard. Sprinkle with grated cheese and season to taste. Roll up each sheet of lasagne, enclosing the ham and cheese filling. Place the rolls in a greased, shallow ovenproof dish. Pour over the mushroom soup and arrange the slices of tomato on top. Bake in a fairly hot oven (190°C/375°F or Gas Mark 5) for 30 minutes. Serve hot garnished with parsley sprigs.

Smoked haddock and egg lasagne

This is a pasta dish with a different taste: lasagne is usually teamed with a meat sauce and a creamy smoked haddock sauce makes a welcome change.

Metric	Imperial
1 × 15 ml spoon vegetable oil	1 tablespoon vegetable oil
175 g lasagne verde	6 oz lasagne verde
450 ml Savoury white sauce (see page 30)	¾ pint Savoury white sauce (see page 30)
100 g Cheddar cheese, grated	¼ lb Cheddar cheese, grated
175 g cooked smoked haddock fillet, skinned, boned and flaked	6 oz cooked smoked haddock fillet, skinned boned and flaked
4 × 15 ml spoons double or single cream	4 tablespoons double or single cream
Salt and freshly ground black pepper	Salt and freshly ground black pepper
3 eggs	3 eggs
25 g butter	1 oz butter

Bring a large pan of lightly salted water to the boil and add the oil. Lower the lasagne, one sheet at a time, into the pan and cook for 5 minutes. Drain well and lay the sheets of lasagne on a large piece of greased greaseproof paper or foil.

Heat the white sauce in a pan with half the grated cheese, the flaked smoked haddock, cream and seasoning. Layer the lasagne and fish sauce in a greased ovenproof dish, starting and finishing with a layer of sauce. Bake in a fairly hot oven (190°C/375°F or Gas Mark 5) for 30 minutes.

Meanwhile, beat the eggs with the seasoning to taste. Melt the butter in a frying pan and add the beaten eggs. Cook, stirring, over a gentle heat until the eggs begin to scramble. Remove from the heat and immediately spoon over the lasagne. Sprinkle with the remaining cheese and return to the oven for a further 10 minutes.

Basic rules for rice cookery

Long-grain rice has always been popular as an accompaniment to curry but has only recently been accepted in more adventurous forms such as risotto or pilaf. Long-grain can form the major ingredient of a main dish and any leftover blends beautifully with simple dressings to make a cold salad. Round-grain rice, for puddings, is usually cooked in milk. The essential rules for cooking rice for savoury dishes are given below.

Basic method

1. Cook rice in a large saucepan in plenty of salted boiling water. The saucepan must be large enough to allow the contents to boil really fast during cooking without boiling over. Do not cover the pan. Test after 12 minutes by squeezing one grain between finger and thumb; it should be quite soft.
2. Drain the cooked rice thoroughly and rinse with fresh hot water to remove any excess rice flour.
3. To dry out the rice, return it to the rinsed-out pan over a moderate heat for 1 minute, shaking the pan occasionally.

Cup method

Take any cup and measure rice in proportion of 1 cup to 2 cups of water and 1 × 5 ml spoon / 1 teaspoon salt. Add the rice to the cold water, bring to the boil and stir once. Lower the heat, cover the pan and simmer without removing the lid or stirring. Test after 15 minutes to see whether all the liquid has been absorbed and the grains of rice are tender. Add a little more water or simply continue cooking, as necessary. When cooked, the rice can easily be fluffed with a fork to separate the grains.

Chicken liver risotto

This is a more elaborate way of cooking rice which keeps the grains beautifully separate because the frying eliminates any loose rice flour surrounding them.

Metric	Imperial
65 g butter	2½ oz butter
1 × 15 ml spoon vegetable oil	1 tablespoon vegetable oil
225 g long-grain rice	½ lb long-grain rice
175 g chicken livers	6 oz chicken livers
175 g button mushrooms, wiped and thinly sliced	6 oz button mushrooms, wiped and thinly sliced
2 × 15 ml spoons tomato purée	2 tablespoons tomato purée
450 ml chicken stock	¾ pint chicken stock
Sprigs of parsley to garnish	Sprigs of parsley to garnish

Heat 50 g/2 oz of the butter and the oil in a non-stick saucepan or one with a heavy base. Add the rice and cook, stirring occasionally, until just transparent.

Meanwhile, toss the chicken livers and sliced mushrooms in the remaining butter until the livers are just firm. Using kitchen scissors, snip up the livers into bite-sized pieces. Add the livers and mushrooms to the rice.

Dissolve the tomato purée in the hot stock, pour over the rice and bring to the boil. Stir gently, reduce the heat, cover and simmer for about 20 minutes, or until the rice is tender and all the liquid has been absorbed. Fluff up and serve hot, garnished with sprigs of parsley. Hand grated Parmesan cheese separately.

Chicken liver risotto

Oven-baked pilaff

This is an alternative to the risotto method which is extremely successful and saves fuel when the oven is in use for cooking another dish.

Metric
350 g boneless raw chicken, finely diced
600 ml chicken stock
25 g butter
1 × 15 ml spoon vegetable oil
25 g flaked almonds
1 × 15 ml spoon pine nuts (optional)
225 g long-grain rice
1 × 2.5 ml spoon ground ginger
1 × 1.25 ml spoon ground cinnamon
Salt and freshly ground black pepper
2 bay leaves

Imperial
12 oz boneless raw chicken, finely diced
1 pint chicken stock
1 oz butter
1 tablespoon vegetable oil
1 oz flaked almonds
1 tablespoon pine nuts (optional)
½ lb long-grain rice
½ teaspoon ground ginger
¼ teaspoon ground cinnamon
Salt and freshly ground black pepper
2 bay leaves

Place the chicken meat in a saucepan and pour over the chicken stock. Bring to the boil, reduce the heat, cover and simmer for 5 minutes. Heat the butter and oil in a clean saucepan and use to fry the flaked almonds and pine nuts, then the rice, stirring until the rice is transparent. Sprinkle in the ground ginger and cinnamon and stir for 1 minute. Add the strained stock from cooking the chicken and bring to the boil. Remove from the heat, stir in the chicken meat, season, and pour the mixture into a greased, shallow casserole. Lay the bay leaves on top.

Cover and cook in a fairly hot oven (190°C/375°F or Gas Mark 5) for 35 minutes, or until all the liquid is absorbed. Remove the bay leaves and fork round lightly before serving.

Oven-baked pilaff

Rice rissoles; Sausage kedgeree

Rice rissoles

This recipe lends itself to many variations. The dill pickles may be replaced with a mixture of chopped fresh parsley and dried sweet herbs, or with the grated zest from oranges and lemons. If liked, a hint of mixed spice can be added too.

Metric	Imperial
350 g lean minced beef	¾ lb lean minced beef
225 g cooked long-grain rice	½ lb cooked long-grain rice
1 large onion, peeled and finely chopped	1 large onion, peeled and finely chopped
50 g Cheddar cheese, grated	2 oz Cheddar cheese, grated
1 × 15 ml spoon chopped dill pickles	1 tablespoon chopped dill pickles
Salt and freshly ground black pepper	Salt and freshly ground black pepper
3 eggs	3 eggs
2 × 15 ml spoons cold water	2 tablespoons cold water
Flour for coating	Flour for coating
Vegetable oil for frying	Vegetable oil for frying

Stir together in a large bowl the minced beef, rice, chopped onion, grated cheese, chopped pickles and seasoning. Break in 2 eggs, mix thoroughly, and form with floured hands into 12 balls. Beat the remaining egg with the water and use to coat the balls. Roll them in flour and refrigerate on a plate, slipped inside a polythene bag for at least 1 hour to become firm.

Fry in deep hot fat (190°C/375°F) (as for Macaroni cheese balls, see page 92) until a rich golden-brown.

Sausage kedgeree

Although kedgeree usually contains fish, this sausage version makes a pleasant alternative.

Metric	Imperial
½ kg chipolata sausages	1 lb chipolata sausages
2 eggs	2 eggs
175 g long-grain rice	6 oz long-grain rice
50 g butter	2 oz butter
Salt and freshly ground black pepper	Salt and freshly ground black pepper
4 × 15 ml spoons chopped parsley	4 tablespoons chopped parsley
Lemon twists to garnish	Lemon twists to garnish

Grill the chipolata sausages until golden-brown on all sides and cooked through. Cut into bite-sized pieces. Put the eggs into cold water, bring to the boil and simmer for 10 minutes. Remove the eggs, lightly crack the shells and plunge them into a bowl of cold water. Cook the long-grain rice in rapidly boiling salted water for about 10 minutes until just tender. Drain thoroughly and toss with a fork to separate the grains. Shell the hard-boiled eggs and chop roughly. Melt the butter in a pan, add the sausage pieces and the cooked rice and season to taste. Add the chopped hard-boiled egg and stir with a fork over a gentle heat for a few minutes, until the kedgeree is heated through. Add half the chopped parsley and pile up on a hot serving dish. Sprinkle with the remaining chopped parsley. Serve hot, garnished with lemon twists.

Puddings, desserts and preserves

We all have favourite baked or steamed puddings of the classic variety. The slightly more unusual recipes included in this chapter, both hot and cold, are planned as treats although they still come into the economy class. Freezer owners might make up twice the quantity of batter for a Yorkshire pudding and leave one half of it unseasoned. If this batter pudding is cooked in melted margarine or butter and allowed to get cold it freezes very well, and can be defrosted and reheated at a later date, when the oven is in use for the main course, to serve as a pudding with golden syrup or a melted jam sauce. Plain rice puddings use up valuable oven heat when one grid would otherwise be left empty and are really delicious served cold with fruit or jam.

Cheesecakes are becoming increasingly popular but can be expensive to make unless the ingredients are chosen with care. An unbaked cheesecake is the obvious economy choice on days when the oven is not in use.

Preserves are no longer cheaper to make at home if soft fruit is affected by the weather, with the result that it never drops in price throughout the season. For this reason this chapter includes a jelly and jam made with wild fruit, or windfall apples which are often given away; and a soft fruit jam combined with rhubarb to give extra bulk at little additional cost, but still retaining the fresh berry taste.

Equally, green tomatoes are often to be had for the asking at the end of the growing season and make a very good uncooked chutney; also a saving on time, trouble and the fuel for cooking.

Apple charlotte with brown breadcrumbs (left);
Five-cup pudding (above)

Apple charlotte with brown breadcrumbs

Here is a more interesting version of Apple charlotte.

Metric	Imperial
½ kg cooking apples, peeled cored and sliced	1 lb cooking apples, peeled cored and sliced
2 × 15 ml spoons water	2 tablespoons water
100 g soft brown sugar	¼ lb soft brown sugar
100 g fresh brown breadcrumbs	¼ lb fresh brown breadcrumbs
2 × 15 ml spoons demerara sugar	2 tablespoons demerara sugar
1 × 2.5 ml spoon ground cinnamon	½ teaspoon ground cinnamon
2 × 15 ml spoons shredded beef suet	2 tablespoons shredded beef suet

Put the sliced apples into a saucepan with the water and simmer for 10 to 15 minutes until tender. Sweeten.

Mix breadcrumbs, demerara sugar and cinnamon.

Place half the sweetened apple in a greased pie dish. Cover with half the crumb mixture, then the rest of the apple and finally top with the remaining crumb mixture. Sprinkle the surface with the shredded suet.

Cover the dish with greased greaseproof paper or foil and bake in a moderate oven (180°C/350°F or Gas Mark 4) for 30 to 40 minutes. Serve very hot with custard or cream.

Five-cup pudding

This is such a useful recipe because the size of the pudding can be varied according to what size cup you use. This one is based on a 200 ml/7 fl oz teacup.

Metric	Imperial
1 × 200 ml teacup self-raising flour	1 × 7 fl oz teacup self-raising flour
1 × 200 ml teacup currants or chopped seedless raisins	1 × 7 fl oz teacup currants or chopped seedless raisins
1 × 200 ml teacup soft brown sugar	1 × 7 fl oz teacup soft brown sugar
1 × 200 ml teacup shredded beef suet	1 × 7 fl oz teacup shredded beef suet
1 × 200 ml teacup milk	1 × 7 fl oz teacup milk
1 × 5 ml spoon ground mixed spice (optional)	1 teaspoon ground mixed spice (optional)

Put all the dry ingredients into a mixing bowl. Add the milk and stir well to mix. Pour the mixture into a well-greased 1 litre/1¾ pint pudding basin leaving a 2.5 cm/1 inch space at the top. Cover the top with greased greaseproof paper or foil, make a pleat in the centre and tie on with string round the rim.

Place the basin in a large pan of gently bubbling water and steam for 3 hours. Remove the basin carefully from the pan, discard the greaseproof paper or foil and turn the pudding out on a hot serving dish. Serve hot with custard.

Rhubarb pudding

Fruit and noodle pudding

Here is a filling pudding which is equally delicious made with golden or red plums or with fresh apricots in spring. The left-overs are just as nice served cold.

Metric	Imperial
225 g broad noodles	½ lb broad noodles
1 large cooking apple, peeled and grated	1 large cooking apple, peeled and grated
100 g soft brown sugar	¼ lb soft brown sugar
1 × 5 ml spoon ground cinnamon	1 teaspoon ground cinnamon
Good pinch of grated nutmeg	Good pinch of grated nutmeg
50 g seedless raisins	2 oz seedless raisins
40 g butter, melted	1½ oz butter, melted
3 eggs, separated	3 eggs, separated

Drop the noodles into a large saucepan of boiling water. Stir gently to keep them separate and cook for about 12 minutes, or until just tender. Drain in a colander, rinse with fresh water, drain again and turn into a large mixing bowl. Stir in the grated apple, sugar, spices, raisins and melted butter. Lightly beat the egg yolks and stir into the noodle mixture. Stiffly whisk the egg whites and fold in gently but thoroughly.

Turn mixture into a well-greased ovenproof dish, cover and bake in a moderate oven (180°C/350°F or Gas Mark 4) for 45 minutes.

Fruit and noodle pudding

Rhubarb pudding

An old-fashioned pudding recipe which can also be used with other fruit such as roughly chopped apples or blackberries. It is useful to cook when the main dish requires an oven with a moderately hot temperature.

Metric	Imperial
100 g self-raising flour	¼ lb self-raising flour
Pinch of salt	Pinch of salt
50 g butter or margarine, cut into pieces	2 oz butter or margarine, cut into pieces
100 g sugar	¼ lb sugar
½ kg young rhubarb, trimmed, cleaned and cut into 2.5 cm slices	1 lb young rhubarb, trimmed, cleaned and cut into 1 inch slices
150 ml milk	¼ pint milk

Sift the flour and salt into a mixing bowl. Add the fat and rub into the flour with the fingertips until the mixture resembles fine breadcrumbs. Stir in the sugar and rhubarb and beat in the milk to make a thick batter. Turn into a buttered 1 litre / 1¾ pint baking dish and bake in a fairly hot oven (200°C/400°F or Gas Mark 6) for 30 to 40 minutes. Serve at once with caster sugar.

Orange treacle tart

Orange treacle tart

A substantial sweet to serve hot or cold with a filling in which breadcrumbs add to the delicious toffee texture.

Metric	Imperial
FOR THE PASTRY:	FOR THE PASTRY:
225 g flour	½ lb flour
Pinch of salt	Pinch of salt
50 g margarine, cut into pieces	2 oz margarine, cut into pieces
50 g lard, cut into pieces	2 oz lard, cut into pieces
2 × 15 ml spoons cold water	2 tablespoons cold water
FOR THE FILLING:	FOR THE FILLING:
225 g golden syrup	½ lb golden syrup
100 g chunky marmalade	¼ lb chunky marmalade
2 × 15 ml spoons lemon juice	2 tablespoons lemon juice
225 g fresh white breadcrumbs	½ lb fresh white breadcrumbs

To make the pastry, sift the flour and salt into a bowl. Rub in the margarine and lard and add just sufficient cold water to make a firm dough. Wrap in foil or greaseproof paper and chill in the refrigerator for 30 minutes.

Roll out the pastry on a floured surface and use to line a 20 cm/8 inch sandwich tin or a flan dish or flan ring placed on a baking sheet.

To make the filling, mix together the syrup, marmalade and lemon juice until well blended. Add the breadcrumbs and stir until coated with the syrup mixture. Spoon the filling into the pastry case and smooth the top. Bake in a moderate oven (180°C/350°F or Gas Mark 4) for 25 to 30 minutes, or until golden-brown.

Pineapple cheese cream

Pineapple cheese cream

This rich-tasting cream dessert owes much of its delicious consistency to the addition of cottage cheese.

Metric	Imperial
1 × 15 ml spoon gelatine	1 tablespoon gelatine
2 × 15 ml spoons hot water	2 tablespoons hot water
1 × 425 g can pineapple chunks	1 × 15 oz can pineapple chunks
2 eggs, separated	2 eggs, separated
100 g caster sugar	¼ lb caster sugar
1 × 15 ml spoon lemon juice and grated zest of ½ lemon	1 tablespoon lemon juice and grated zest of ½ lemon
350 g cottage cheese, sieved	¾ lb cottage cheese, sieved
150 ml double cream	¼ pint double cream
Angelica leaves to decorate	Angelica leaves to decorate

Soften the gelatine in the water. Drain the syrup from the pineapple chunks. Whisk the egg yolks and sugar together until thick and creamy. Slowly whisk in 150 ml/¼ pint pineapple syrup.

Put the mixture into a saucepan, add the softened gelatine and stir over low heat until dissolved. Add the grated lemon zest and leave to cool. Stir in the sieved cottage cheese and lemon juice. Leave until beginning to set. Beat until smooth.

Lightly whip the cream and fold into the mixture. Beat the egg whites until stiff, and finely chop half the pineapple chunks. Fold the chopped pineapple and the beaten egg whites into the mixture. Put into a serving dish or individual glasses, and decorate with the remaining pineapple chunks and angelica leaves. Chill before serving.

Christmas crumble

The richness of the mincemeat with the contrast in textures make this the 'leftovers' sweet for a special occasion.

Metric	Imperial
100 g mincemeat	*¼ lb mincemeat*
150 ml cold water	*¼ pint cold water*
Finely grated zest of 1 orange	*Finely grated zest of 1 orange*
2 × 5 ml spoons cornflour	*2 teaspoons cornflour*
1 × 15 ml spoon rum or brandy	*1 tablespoon rum or brandy*
2 × 5 ml spoons sugar	*2 teaspoons sugar*
FOR THE TOPPING:	FOR THE TOPPING:
100 g butter	*¼ lb butter*
50 g demerara sugar	*2 oz demerara sugar*
100 g quick cook oats	*¼ lb quick cook oats*
TO DECORATE:	TO DECORATE:
150 ml double cream	*¼ pint double cream*
25 g chopped walnuts	*1 oz chopped walnuts*

Place the mincemeat with the cold water and orange zest in a saucepan. Bring to the boil, reduce the heat and simmer for 5 minutes. Moisten the cornflour with 1 × 15 ml spoon / 1 tablespoon of water and stir it into the mincemeat, then add the rum or brandy and the sugar. Bring to the boil, stirring constantly. Cook for 1 minute then allow to become quite cold.

To make the topping, melt the butter in a saucepan and stir in the demerara sugar and oats until well coated. Place half the oat mixture in the bottom of a trifle dish, cover with the mincemeat sauce and top with the remaining oat mixture.

Whip the cream until just holding its shape then spread lightly over the centre of the crumble and sprinkle with the chopped walnuts.

Christmas crumble

Cold rice crème; Fruit slices

Fruit slices

The cooked filling in these pastry slices is thickened with cornflour to make it go further but the flavour is surprisingly rich.

Metric	Imperial
FOR THE PASTRY:	FOR THE PASTRY:
225 g flour	*½ lb flour*
Pinch of salt	*Pinch of salt*
150 g butter or margarine, cut into pieces	*5 oz butter or margarine, cut into pieces*
2 × 5 ml spoons caster sugar	*2 teaspoons caster sugar*
2–3 × 15 ml spoons cold water	*2–3 tablespoons cold water*
FOR THE FILLING:	FOR THE FILLING:
1 × 15 ml spoon cornflour	*1 tablespoon cornflour*
150 ml water	*¼ pint water*
75 g sugar	*3 oz sugar*
350 g mixed dried fruit (sultanas, raisins, currants)	*¾ lb mixed dried fruit (sultanas, raisins, currants)*
1 × 5 ml spoon ground cinnamon	*1 teaspoon ground cinnamon*
TO GLAZE:	TO GLAZE:
Cold water	*Cold water*
Caster sugar	*Caster sugar*

Sift the flour and salt into a bowl. Rub in the fat with the fingertips until the mixture resembles fine breadcrumbs. Stir in the sugar and add just sufficient water to hold the mixture together, then form into a smooth ball. Wrap in foil or greaseproof paper and chill in the refrigerator for 30 minutes.

To make the filling, blend the cornflour to a smooth paste with a little of the water. Stir in the remaining water and place in a saucepan. Add the sugar, fruit and cinnamon and bring to the boil, stirring constantly, until the mixture thickens. Cook for 1 minute then allow to cool.

Divide the pastry into 2 equal portions. Roll out one half to line a greased 30 × 22.5 cm / 12 × 9 inch Swiss roll tin. Cover the base with the fruit mixture and spread evenly. Roll the remaining pastry to cover. Lay this over the filling, dampen the edges and press together to seal. Flute with your finger and thumb or press with the back of a fork. Brush with a little water and dredge with caster sugar. Bake in a fairly hot oven (190°C/375°F or Gas Mark 5) for about 25 minutes, or until pale golden.

Cut into 5 × 11 cm / 2 × 4½ inch slices and allow to cool before removing from the tin.

Makes 12

Cold rice crème

Although hot rice pudding with plenty of jam makes a fine winter dessert, it should not be overlooked that rice may also be used as the basis for attractive summer sweets.

Metric	Imperial
75 g round-grain rice	*3 oz round-grain rice*
600 ml milk	*1 pint milk*
25 g sugar	*1 oz sugar*
1 egg, separated	*1 egg, separated*
15 g butter	*½ oz butter*
1 packet orange jelly	*1 packet orange jelly*
Few glacé cherries,	*Few glacé cherries,*
halved, to decorate	*halved, to decorate*

Put the rice, milk and sugar in a saucepan. Bring to the boil, stir well, reduce the heat, cover and simmer for 30 minutes, stirring occasionally. Lightly beat the egg yolk, stir into the rice mixture with the butter, then remove from the heat. Dissolve the jelly in 150 ml / ¼ pint boiling water and allow to cool. Stir into the rice mixture. Whisk the egg white until stiff and fold into the rice and jelly mixture, then pour into an oiled ring mould. Chill well until set. Turn out on a serving dish and decorate with halved glacé cherries.

Delicate orange pudding

Delicate orange pudding

This is a light pudding with a fresh, fruity flavour which is easy to turn out and looks extremely tempting.

Metric	Imperial
100 g glacé cherries	¼ lb glacé cherries
50 g angelica	2 oz angelica
100 g unsalted butter	¼ lb unsalted butter
100 g caster sugar	¼ lb caster sugar
Grated zest and juice of 1 orange	Grated rind and juice of 1 orange
2 eggs, beaten	2 eggs, beaten
75 g self-raising flour	3 oz self-raising flour
50 g fresh white breadcrumbs	2 oz fresh white breadcrumbs
3 × 15 ml spoons lemon jelly marmalade	3 tablespoons lemon jelly marmalade
1 orange, peeled and thinly sliced	1 orange, peeled and thinly sliced

Roughly chop the glacé cherries and angelica. Soften the butter slightly and cream with the sugar until light and fluffy. Add the orange zest. Gradually beat in the eggs. Sift the flour, mix with the breadcrumbs and fold into the creamed mixture. Stir in the orange juice, cherries and angelica to distribute the fruit evenly through the mixture.

Coat the base and sides of a 1 kg / 2 lb loaf tin with the jelly marmalade and cover with overlapping orange slices. Pour the pudding mixture into the tin. Stand it in a roasting tin, half filled with water, and bake in a fairly hot oven (200°C/400°F or Gas Mark 6) for 45 minutes.

Turn out on a serving dish and serve hot with custard or lightly whipped cream.

Mocha mousse

This adaptable mousse can be set in small individual moulds, even coffee cups, instead of one large mould. It is much more economical than a mousse made with melted chocolate for instance, but just as delicious.

Metric	Imperial
1 × 15 ml spoon gelatine	1 tablespoon gelatine
2 × 15 ml spoons cold water	2 tablespoons cold water
2 × 15 ml spoons instant coffee	2 tablespoons instant coffee
1 × 15 ml spoon cocoa powder	1 tablespoon cocoa powder
2 × 15 ml spoons sugar	2 tablespoons sugar
300 ml boiling water	½ pint boiling water
200 ml evaporated milk, chilled	7 fl.oz. evaporated milk, chilled
TO DECORATE:	TO DECORATE:
4 × 15 ml spoons double cream, whipped (optional)	4 tablespoons double cream, whipped (optional)
Chocolate curls (optional)	Chocolate curls (optional)

Sprinkle the gelatine over the cold water in a cup and allow to soften for 5 minutes.

Place the instant coffee, cocoa and sugar in a measuring jug and gradually add the boiling water, stirring all the time until dissolved. Add the softened gelatine and stir well until completely melted. Allow to cool until mixture is on the point of setting.

Place the evaporated milk in a bowl and whisk steadily until it is thick and fluffy. Gradually whisk in the coffee mixture and pour into a rinsed 1 litre / 1¾ pint fluted mould. Chill until set then turn out on a serving dish. If liked, decorate with rosettes of whipped cream and chocolate curls.

Chocolate curls
These can be made quickly by scraping a clean potato peeler across the bottom of a block of plain chocolate.

Chocolate chews

A delightful sticky sweet treat for children.

Metric	Imperial
50 g caster sugar	2 oz caster sugar
2 × 15 ml spoons golden syrup	2 tablespoons golden syrup
75 g butter	3 oz butter
225 g quick cook oats	½ lb quick cook oats
3 × 15 ml spoons cocoa powder	3 tablespoons cocoa powder
1 × 5 ml spoon vanilla or rum essence	1 teaspoon vanilla or rum essence
25 g walnuts, chopped	1 oz walnuts, chopped
50 g seedless raisins, chopped	2 oz seedless raisins, chopped

Place the sugar, syrup and butter in a saucepan. Stir over gentle heat until the sugar has dissolved. Bring the mixture

Mocha mousse

to the boil, remove from the heat and stir in the oats, cocoa powder, vanilla or rum essence, chopped walnuts and chopped raisins.

Mix very thoroughly and spread in a buttered 20 cm / 8 inch square cake tin. Chill in the refrigerator until firm then cut into 5 cm / 2 inch squares. Remove from the tin with a palette knife and store in an airtight container. **Makes 16**

Unbaked apricot cheesecake

A flan ring placed on a baking sheet can be used instead of the loose-bottomed cake tin for this recipe. The cheesecake needs no decoration but could be served scattered with toasted flaked almonds.

Metric	Imperial
FOR THE BISCUIT CRUST:	FOR THE BISCUIT CRUST:
50 g butter or margarine	*2 oz butter or margarine*
100 g digestive biscuits, crushed	*¼ lb digestive biscuits, crushed*
1 × 2.5 ml spoon ground cinnamon	*½ teaspoon ground cinnamon*
FOR THE FILLING:	FOR THE FILLING:
1 × 425 g can apricot halves	*1 × 15 oz can apricot halves*
350 g cottage cheese, sieved	*¾ lb cottage cheese, sieved*
75 g caster sugar	*3 oz caster sugar*
Grated zest and juice of 1 large lemon	*Grated zest and juice of 1 large lemon*
1 × 15 ml spoon gelatine	*1 tablespoon gelatine*
150 ml whipping cream	*¼ pint whipping cream*
Flaked almonds (optional)	*Flaked almonds (optional)*

Place the butter or margarine in a saucepan. Stir over moderate heat until just melted, but do not allow it to colour. Remove from the heat, stir in the biscuit crumbs and ground cinnamon and mix well. Press the crumb mixture into the base of a greased loose-bottomed 17.5 cm / 7 inch cake tin, smoothing well with the back of a metal spoon. Chill in the refrigerator while preparing the filling.

Drain the apricot halves, reserve the syrup, and liquidize in an electric blender or pass through a sieve. Place the apricot purée, sieved cottage cheese, sugar and lemon zest and juice together in a bowl and beat until smooth. Measure 2 × 15 ml spoons / 2 tablespoons of the reserved apricot syrup in a small basin, sprinkle on the gelatine and stir well. Place the basin in a pan of hot water and stir until the gelatine has completely dissolved. Cool and add to the cheese mixture. Whip the cream until thick and fold into the cheese mixture. Turn on to the chilled biscuit base and allow to set. Remove the cake tin and serve the cheesecake on its base on a plate. If liked, sprinkle with flaked almonds.

Unbaked apricot cheesecake; Chocolate chews

Crab apple jelly

A delicious deep pink jelly well worth making if you know of a local source of this fruit. If not, use small unripe windfall apples.

Metric	Imperial
Crab apples	Crab apples
Water	Water
Sugar	Sugar
Lemons	Lemons

Wash the apples, remove any blemished parts and cut them in half. Place in a preserving pan or large saucepan and just cover with water. Bring to the boil and simmer until reduced to a soft pulp. Strain through a jelly bag overnight but do not squeeze the bag or the jelly will be cloudy.

Measure the crab apple juice and place in a preserving pan. Add ½ kg / 1 lb sugar and the thinly pared rind of half a lemon to each 600 ml / 1 pint of crab apple juice. Bring slowly to the boil, stirring until the sugar has dissolved. Boil rapidly, skimming if necessary, until the jelly will set when tested.

To test for setting, first remove the pan from the heat. Place a small quantity of jelly on a small plate, cool, then push gently with a fingertip. If the surface wrinkles the jelly is ready.

Have ready sufficient warm dry sterilized jars on a board, and ladle in the jam. Cover at once with waxed paper discs and cling wrap covers. Label the jars.

The lemon rind may be removed before potting or one piece added to each jar of jelly as preferred.

Crab apple jam

This may be made with the pulp remaining in the jelly bag after making Crab apple jelly.

Metric	Imperial
Crab apple pulp	Crab apple pulp
Water	Water
Sugar	Sugar
Cloves	Cloves
Pared lemon rind tied in a piece of muslin	Pared lemon rind tied in a piece of muslin

Measure the pulp and place in a preserving pan or large saucepan. Add 2 × 15 ml spoons / 2 tablespoons water to each 600 ml / 1 pint of pulp and bring to the boil. Sieve. Measure the sieved pulp and return to the pan.

To every 600 ml / 1 pint of pulp add ½ kg / 1 lb sugar, 2 cloves and the rind of half a lemon. Bring to the boil stirring occasionally to dissolve the sugar. Boil rapidly until setting point is reached. Test as for Crab apple jelly. Remove the muslin bag of flavouring.

Ladle the jam into the prepared sterilized jars as for Crab apple jelly. Cover at once with waxed paper discs and cling wrap covers. Label the jars.

Crab apple jam; Crab apple jelly; Strawberry and rhubarb jam

Strawberry and rhubarb jam

Soft berry fruits for home-made jams are not cheap to buy, and are rarely plentiful enough in the garden to make more than a few pounds of preserves. By combining them with rhubarb, which has a bland flavour, fruits such as strawberries and raspberries go further, and produce a very richly flavoured jam.

Metric	Imperial
1 kg rhubarb, leaves and base trimmed from the stalks	2 lb rhubarb, leaves and base trimmed from the stalks
150 ml water	¼ pint water
3 × 15 ml spoons lemon juice	3 tablespoons lemon juice
1 kg strawberries, hulled	2 lb strawberries, hulled
2 kg preserving sugar	4 lb preserving sugar
15 g butter	½ oz butter
1 bottle liquid pectin	1 bottle liquid pectin

Uncooked green tomato chutney

The long boiling process necessary when making conventional chutney costs money in fuel, and fills the kitchen with steam. For long-term freezer storage, or up to one week after opening in the refrigerator, an uncooked chutney is quick to make and keeps perfectly.

Metric	Imperial
1 kg green or small tomatoes, halved or quartered	2 lb green or small tomatoes, halved or quartered
¾ kg mild onions, peeled and finely chopped	1½ lb mild onions, peeled and finely chopped
100 g sultanas	¼ lb sultanas
150 g seedless raisins	5 oz seedless raisins
100 g soft brown sugar	¼ lb soft brown sugar
1 × 15 ml spoon salt	1 tablespoon salt
1 × 15 ml spoon dry mustard	1 tablespoon dry mustard
1 × 2.5 ml spoon ground ginger	½ teaspoon ground ginger
1 × 2.5 ml spoon cayenne pepper	½ teaspoon cayenne pepper
Malt vinegar	Malt vinegar

Mince the tomatoes and chopped onion, and place in a bowl. Add the dried fruit, sugar, salt, mustard, ground ginger and cayenne pepper and mix together thoroughly. Leave to stand for 2 hours to allow the flavours to develop and blend well.

Pack into sterilized jars, leaving a 2.5 cm/1 inch headspace. Just cover the contents of each jar with cold vinegar. Seal with cling wrap covers and either place in the freezer or refrigerate. Unopened, the chutney will keep in the refrigerator for 3 months, once opened it should be used up in one week.

Makes approx. 2 kg/4 lb

Uncooked green tomato chutney

Cut the rhubarb stalks into 2.5 cm/1 inch lengths. Place in a preserving pan with the water and lemon juice. Bring slowly to the boil, simmer for 5 minutes, allow to cool. Add the strawberries, cutting the larger fruit in half. Add the sugar. Allow to stand for 1 hour, stirring occasionally. Place over a low heat and stir continuously until the sugar has dissolved. Add the butter to reduce foaming, bring to a full rolling boil, and boil rapidly for 5 minutes. Remove from the heat, add the pectin and stir well.

Allow to cool for 20 minutes before potting to prevent the fruit from rising to the top of the jars. Have ready sufficient warm, dry, sterilized jars on a board, and pour in the jam. Allow to get completely cold, cover with waxed paper discs and cling wrap covers. Label the jars.

Yields 3 kg/6–7 lb jam
Variation
Jam can be made in the same way with raspberries instead of strawberries, but as they have a better setting power than strawberries, reduce both the lemon juice and liquid pectin in proportion. You can also use diced marrow flesh or pumpkin flesh to make mixed fruit jams, but make sure the diced flesh is sufficiently tender before adding the berry fruit and sugar.

Delicious home baking

There is no doubt that home-made bread costs less than the ready-baked variety, but it is entirely a personal decision whether you wish to save the time involved for other things, and therefore would not find the saving in money worth while. For those who really enjoy a baking session in the kitchen it is very satisfying, especially when you can count on producing a number of different loaves and fancy rolls from one batch of dough. For those who enjoy pizzas, white bread dough can be formed in a thin round, to fit the plate of your choice, spread with a savoury tomato sauce, then topped with anchovies and grated cheese, or crumbled cooked bacon and chopped olives. When risen, pizzas can be baked in 20 to 30 minutes, according to size and thickness. Those not immediately eaten are very good for freezing.

Family baking extends far beyond the making of yeasted bread. With some experience you can prepare teabreads and scones of many varieties very quickly. They take little time to bake and are usually best eaten fresh, and even hot. Cakes should be capable of maturing and improving as they are frequently not eaten up on the day they are made, so the recipes given here are for cakes that will taste just as good, or even better, if properly stored, for up to a week.

Those choux pastry delicacies which cost so much to buy, are much easier to make than you would think. When recipes for fillings are provided as well, they become treats which are surprisingly inexpensive compared with those bought ready-made.

Basic brown or white bread

From the following amount of basic bread dough you can make one large loaf and two smaller loaves, or one large loaf and a selection of smaller breads or shaped rolls. Brown or white flour can be used according to preference.

Metric	Imperial
15 g dried yeast	*½ oz dried yeast*
2 × 15 ml spoons soft brown sugar	*2 tablespoons soft brown sugar*
900 ml water	*1½ pints water*
1 × 15 ml spoon salt	*1 tablespoon salt*
1½ kg strong white or wholewheat flour	*3 lb strong white or wholewheat flour*
25 g butter	*1 oz butter*
1 egg, beaten with a pinch of salt	*1 egg, beaten with a pinch of salt*

Put the dried yeast into a small basin with 1 × 5 ml spoon / 1 teaspoon of the sugar. Heat the water to 50°C/110°F. (If the water is too cool, the dough will not rise properly.) Whisk 300 ml / ½ pint of the warm water into the dried yeast and sugar. Leave in a warm place for 10 to 15 minutes, until the surface is covered with bubbles. Add the salt and the remaining sugar to the rest of the warm water.

Any of the following three methods can be used for mixing the dough:

1. Put the flour into a large mixing bowl and rub in the butter. Pour in both the salt water and the yeast liquid. Quickly work the flour and liquid together to a dough with the fingertips. If the mixture seems dry, add a little more water. Knead the dough for 5 minutes until smooth, pulling the outside dough into the centre.

2. Put the flour into a pile on a clean working surface and rub in the butter. Make a large well in the centre of the flour and carefully pour in both the salt water and yeast liquid. Using a round-bladed knife, flick the flour from the sides into the liquid in the centre, mixing with the fingertips as you go. When the liquid has absorbed enough flour to become sticky, work in the rest of the flour. Knead for 5 minutes.

3. Using an electric mixer, put the flour into the mixer bowl with the butter, salt water and yeast liquid. Mix on a slow speed, using the dough hook attachment, until the liquid is absorbed. Continue mixing for 2 minutes, instead of kneading by hand.

Put the kneaded dough into a greased mixing bowl and cover with a damp cloth. Leave in a warm place for about 45 minutes. The dough should double in size.

Turn out the risen dough on a floured working surface and knead lightly, using as little flour as possible. The dough is now ready for shaping.

Loaves

Divide the dough in half and keep one half warm. Knead the other portion of dough into a smooth ball and punch into a shape to fit a 1 kg/2 lb loaf tin. Put into the warmed and greased tin.

Divide the remaining dough into 2 and shape for 2 ½ kg/1 lb loaf tins. Put into the warmed and greased tins. Brush the loaves with the beaten egg mixture. If using a wholewheat dough, sprinkle with a little cracked wheat or bran.

Put the loaves in a warm, draught-free place and cover with polythene bags. Leave to rise for 20 minutes until the dough reaches the top of the tins. Bake the loaves in a very hot oven (230°C/450°F or Gas Mark 8) for 20 minutes, then reduce the heat to fairly hot (200°C/400°F or Gas Mark 6) for a further 20 minutes for the large loaf, and 10 minutes for the smaller loaves. Tip the loaves out of their tins and tap them on the bottom – the loaves should sound hollow if they are cooked. Cool on a wire rack.

Rolls

Divide the dough into 50 g/2 oz portions, and roll under a cupped hand on a lightly floured surface until round and smooth. Arrange on greased baking sheets and brush with a little beaten egg mixture. The rolls can be sprinkled with sesame, poppy or caraway seeds, or bran. Cover with polythene bags and leave in a warm place to rise for 10 to 15 minutes. Bake in a very hot oven (230°C/450°F or Gas Mark 8) for 10 to 15 minutes.

Makes approx. 40 rolls

NOTE: Fresh yeast can be used in place of dried – 25 g/1 oz fresh yeast is equivalent to 15 g/½ oz dried yeast.

Cottage loaf

This is without doubt one of the most popular breads as far as shape is concerned. Instead of making one large cottage loaf, you can make several smaller ones to serve in place of rolls. These have particular appeal for children.

Metric	Imperial
1½ kg risen bread dough	*3 lb risen bread dough*

Cut off about one quarter of the dough for the 'knob' of the cottage loaf. Knead the larger piece of dough into a smooth, even round and put it on a greased baking sheet. Form the smaller piece of dough into a smooth even ball. Brush the top of the larger piece of dough with water and put the 'knob' centrally on top. Fix in position by pressing the floured handle of a wooden spoon right through the centre to the base of the bottom piece of dough, pulling the spoon handle out carefully.

Cover the shaped loaf with a large polythene bag and leave in a warm place for about 30 minutes until it has risen. The dough should seem light and spongy.

Dredge the top very lightly with flour. Bake in a very hot oven (230°C/450°F or Gas Mark 8) for 15 minutes, then reduce the heat to moderate (180°C/350°F or Gas Mark 4) for a further 20 minutes. Cool on a wire rack.

Individual cottage loaves: Use 75 g/3 oz risen dough for each loaf, breaking off a portion for the knob. Mould as above, but only bake for the first 15 minutes.

Cheese and poppy seed pinwheels

Sugared bun cluster

Cheese and poppy seed pinwheels

These bread knots look rather like small savoury Chelsea buns and they make a tasty accompaniment to serve with soup.

Metric	Imperial
½ kg risen bread dough	1 lb risen bread dough
1 egg, beaten with a pinch of salt	1 egg, beaten with a pinch of salt
25 g grated Parmesan cheese	1 oz grated Parmesan cheese
Poppy seeds	Poppy seeds

Divide the risen bread dough into 12 even-sized portions. Roll each piece into a long thin sausage shape, and flatten lightly with the palm of the hand. Brush each strip of dough with the beaten egg mixture and sprinkle with a little grated Parmesan cheese. Roll up each strip of dough tightly, pressing the ends of the dough to seal.

Stand the pinwheels on greased baking sheets, leaving space for spreading. Brush each pinwheel with the beaten egg mixture and sprinkle the tops with poppy seeds.

Cover with a large polythene bag and leave in a warm place for about 20 minutes until risen. Bake in a hot oven (220°C/425°F or Gas Mark 7) for 15 minutes.

Makes 12

Sugared bun cluster

Based on a basic bread dough, this sticky bun cluster makes a tasty tea-time treat.

Metric	Imperial
½ kg risen bread dough	1 lb risen bread dough
Demerara sugar	Demerara sugar
Milk	Milk
4 × 15 ml spoons honey, melted	4 tablespoons honey, melted
25 g chopped or flaked nuts	1 oz chopped or flaked nuts

Divide the bread dough into 8 even-sized portions. Work a little demerara sugar into each portion of dough, kneading it gently on a very lightly floured surface, to form a smooth ball. Arrange the shaped pieces of dough in a greased 20 cm/8 inch sandwich tin, so that they just touch.

Cover the tin with a large polythene bag and leave in a warm place for about 20 minutes until risen.

Brush the top of the bun cluster with milk. Spoon over the melted honey and sprinkle the surface with extra demerara sugar and the nuts. Bake in a very hot oven (230°C/450°F or Gas Mark 8) for 15 minutes, then reduce the heat to fairly hot (200°C/400°F or Gas Mark 6) for a further 10 minutes. Carefully turn out the bun cluster on a wire rack and allow to cool.

Makes 8

Baps

Extra yeast is added to the basic bread dough to make the baps really light in texture. They also rise and prove more quickly.

Metric
Ingredients as for basic
  white bread dough
1 × 5 ml spoon dried yeast

Imperial
Ingredients as for basic
  white bread dough
1 teaspoon dried yeast

Make up the basic bread dough as on page 108, using the extra dried yeast, and leave to rise.

Divide the risen dough into 75 g/3 oz portions. Form each piece into a smooth ball and roll it into a flat round on a lightly floured surface. Arrange the shaped baps on floured baking sheets, leaving space between each one to allow for spreading.

Cover with a large polythene bag and leave in a warm place for about 20 minutes until risen. The baps should be light and fluffy. Press the floured handle of a wooden spoon into the centre of each bap, and then dredge the tops lightly with flour. Bake in a hot oven (220°C/425°F or Gas Mark 7) for 10 minutes. Cool the cooked baps between folded clean tea towels so that they keep a soft, spongy texture.
Makes approx. 30

Baps

Rye bread

Rye bread

This dark bread is flavoured and coloured with wholewheat flour and black treacle.

Metric
25 g dried yeast
2 × 15 ml spoons black
  treacle
900 ml water
1 × 15 ml spoon salt
1 kg wholewheat flour
½ kg rye flour
25 g butter
1 egg, beaten with a pinch
  of salt
Cracked wheat or bran

Imperial
1 oz dried yeast
2 tablespoons black treacle
1½ pints water
1 tablespoon salt
2 lb wholewheat flour
1 lb rye flour
1 oz butter
1 egg, beaten with a pinch
  of salt
Cracked wheat or bran

Make the rye bread dough as for the basic white bread dough, using the mixed wholewheat and rye flours, and the black treacle in place of the sugar. Allow the dough to rise for 45 minutes and then knead lightly.

Divide the risen dough into 2 equal portions. Shape each one into a long, oval loaf. Put the shaped loaves on greased baking sheets, brush the surface with the beaten egg mixture and sprinkle with cracked wheat or bran.

Make several diagonal cuts in the surface of the loaves with a sharp knife. These cuts allow the loaves to rise or 'bloom' well, hence the name 'bloomer'. Bake in a very hot oven (230°C/450°F or Gas Mark 8) for 20 minutes, then reduce the heat to fairly hot (200°C/400°F or Gas Mark 6) for a further 20 minutes.

Ginger and peanut loaf

This spiced loaf can be eaten plain as a cake, or cut into slices and buttered. Any stale slices can be toasted and eaten like teacakes. Peanuts add an interesting flavour, and, unlike most nuts, they do not make this an expensive recipe.

Metric	Imperial
350 g self-raising flour	¾ lb self-raising flour
Pinch of salt	Pinch of salt
1 × 5 ml spoon ground ginger	1 teaspoon ground ginger
50 g soft brown sugar	2 oz soft brown sugar
75 g sultanas	3 oz sultanas
50 g preserved stem ginger, chopped	2 oz preserved stem ginger, chopped
75 g unsalted peanuts	3 oz unsalted peanuts
75 g butter	3 oz butter
4 × 15 ml spoons black treacle	4 tablespoons black treacle
2 eggs	2 eggs
150 ml milk	¼ pint milk

Grease a 1 kg/2 lb loaf tin and line the base with a piece of greased greaseproof paper. Sift the flour, salt and ground ginger together into a bowl. Add the sugar, sultanas, stem ginger and peanuts.

Put the butter and treacle into a saucepan and heat gently until melted. Add the treacle mixture to the dry ingredients, and gradually beat in the eggs and the milk until well blended. Pour the mixture into the prepared loaf tin and bake in a warm oven (160°C/325°F or Gas Mark 3) for 1¼ hours.

Allow the loaf to cool slightly and then turn out on a wire rack and strip off the lining paper. The loaf can be topped with glacé icing and extra stem ginger and peanuts, if liked.

Ginger and peanut loaf

Wholewheat popover rolls

Wholewheat popover rolls

These tall, flower-pot shaped rolls have a delicious, nutty texture and flavour, and they are particularly good eaten warm with butter and jam or honey.

Metric	Imperial
½ kg risen wholewheat bread dough	1 lb risen wholewheat bread dough
1 egg, beaten with a pinch of salt	1 egg, beaten with a pinch of salt
Cracked wheat or bran	Cracked wheat or bran

Brush the insides of 12 small dariole moulds or castle pudding tins with melted butter. Divide the risen wholewheat bread dough into 12 even-sized portions and drop into the prepared tins.

Cover with a large polythene bag and leave in a warm place for about 20 minutes until risen. Brush the tops of the popovers with the beaten egg mixture and sprinkle with a little cracked wheat or bran. Bake in a hot oven (220°C/425°F or Gas Mark 7) for 15 to 20 minutes until well risen and golden-brown. Turn the popover rolls out of their tins and tap the bottoms to see that they are cooked. Cool on a wire rack.
Makes 12

Rich bran fruit loaf

Edam tea ring

Rich bran fruit loaf

A very easily prepared loaf which is best eaten when freshly baked. Most of the ingredients need to be prepared the night before cooking.

Metric	Imperial
225 g soft brown sugar	*½ lb soft brown sugar*
100 g All Bran	*¼ lb All Bran*
225 g mixed dried fruit (currants, raisins, sultanas)	*½ lb mixed dried fruit (currants, raisins, sultanas)*
1 × 15 ml spoon shredded dried orange peel (see page 14)	*1 tablespoon shredded dried orange peel (see page 14)*
1 × 15 ml spoon golden syrup	*1 tablespoon golden syrup*
250 ml milk	*8 fl oz milk*
1 egg, beaten	*1 egg, beaten*
1 large banana, peeled and mashed	*1 large banana, peeled and mashed*
100 g self-raising flour	*¼ lb self-raising flour*

Place the sugar, All bran, dried fruit, orange peel, syrup and milk in a bowl and stir well. Allow to soak overnight.

The next day, add the beaten egg, mashed banana and flour and mix thoroughly.

Turn the mixture into a greased 1 kg/2 lb loaf tin and bake in a moderate oven (180°C/350°F or Gas Mark 4) for about 1 hour, until the cake is cooked, or until a skewer inserted in the centre comes out clean.

Turn out on a wire rack to cool slightly. Slice the loaf while still warm or very fresh, and serve with butter.

Edam tea ring

Light, cheesy rolls, to serve split and buttered or with savoury fillings.

Metric	Imperial
225 g plain flour	*½ lb plain flour*
4 × 5 ml spoons plus 1 × 2.5 ml spoon baking powder	*4½ teaspoons baking powder*
1 × 5 ml spoon salt	*1 teaspoon salt*
1 × 5 ml spoon paprika	*1 teaspoon paprika*
225 g Edam cheese, grated	*½ lb Edam cheese, grated*
4 × 15 ml spoons piccalilli pickle, chopped	*4 tablespoons piccalilli pickle, chopped*
1 large egg	*1 large egg*
150 ml milk	*¼ pint milk*

Sift the flour, baking powder, salt and paprika pepper into a large mixing bowl. Rub in 200 g/7 oz of the grated cheese and add piccalilli pickle.

Beat the egg and milk together. Pour most of the milk mixture into the cheese mixture, reserving a little for glazing.

Divide the dough into 6 pieces, and form each into a roll. Place these on a baking tray to form a circle, leaving a space between each roll. Brush the rolls with the milk and egg mixture and sprinkle with the remaining cheese.

Bake in a hot oven (220°C/425°F or Gas Mark 7) for 25 minutes.

Cool on a wire rack. Serve as a circle, or broken up, either hot or cold.

113

Drop scones; Welsh cakes; Potato and onion cakes

Griddle scones and cakes

There are two basic types of scones/cakes suitable for cooking on a griddle – those based on a batter, and those based on a shaped and rolled-out mixture. Both can be either sweet or savoury. In some parts of the country these are called girdle scones and cakes.

Drop scones

Metric	Imperial
100 g self-raising flour	*¼ lb self-raising flour*
Pinch of salt	*Pinch of salt*
25 g sugar	*1 oz sugar*
1 egg	*1 egg*
150 ml milk	*¼ pint milk*
25 g butter, melted	*1 oz butter, melted*
Vegetable oil or fat for greasing the griddle	*Vegetable oil or fat for greasing the griddle*

Sift the flour and salt together into a bowl. Stir in the sugar. Add the egg and milk and beat to a smooth batter. Stir in the melted butter to keep the scones moist.

Grease and warm a griddle or heavy-based frying pan. The griddle is hot enough when a little of the mixture dropped on it turns golden underneath in 30 seconds.

Drop the mixture in spoonfuls (1 × 15 ml spoon / 1 tablespoon) on to the hot griddle, allowing space for spreading, and cook for about 2 minutes. When the scones are slightly puffed and covered with bubbles, turn them over to brown the other side.

Keep the first batch of scones wrapped in a clean tea towel, to prevent them drying out, while you cook the rest. Serve hot with butter, jam or honey.

Makes approx 14

Savoury drop scones:
Omit the sugar, and add 1 small grated onion, 1 × 5 ml spoon / 1 teaspoon dry mustard and 50 g / 2 oz grated Parmesan cheese to the batter. Cook as above. Savoury drop scones make an unusual accompaniment to soups.

Welsh cakes

Metric	Imperial
225 g self-raising flour	*½ lb self-raising flour*
Pinch of salt	*Pinch of salt*
100 g butter	*¼ lb butter*
50 g sugar	*2 oz sugar*
50 g currants	*2 oz currants*
25 g chopped nuts	*1 oz chopped nuts*
1 egg	*1 egg*
2 × 15 ml spoons milk	*2 tablespoons milk*
Vegetable oil or fat for greasing the griddle	*Vegetable oil or fat for greasing the griddle*

Sift the flour and salt together into a bowl. Rub in the butter until the mixture resembles fine breadcrumbs. Add the sugar, currants and chopped nuts and mix to a fairly stiff dough with the egg and the milk. Knead the dough lightly on a floured surface and roll out until about 5 mm / ¼ inch thick. Cut into 5 cm / 2 inch rounds with a biscuit cutter.

Grease and warm a griddle or heavy-based frying pan. The griddle is hot enough when a piece of the mixture placed on it turns golden-brown underneath in 30 seconds.

Cook the Welsh cakes for 2 to 3 minutes on each side. Serve warm with plenty of butter.

Makes 8 to 10

Potato and onion cakes

These are a delicious savoury version of Welsh cakes, made and cooked in exactly the same way. They are delicious served with crisply fried bacon.

Metric	Imperial
225 g self-raising flour	½ lb self-raising flour
Pinch of salt	Pinch of salt
1 × 5 ml spoon dry mustard	1 teaspoon dry mustard
100 g butter	¼ lb butter
1 small onion, peeled and grated	1 small onion, peeled and grated
1 large potato, peeled and grated	1 large potato, peeled and grated
2 × 15 ml spoons chopped parsley	2 tablespoons chopped parsley
50 g Cheddar cheese, grated	2 oz Cheddar cheese, grated
1 egg	1 egg
2 × 15 ml spoons milk	2 tablespoons milk
Vegetable oil or fat for greasing the griddle	Vegetable oil or fat for greasing the griddle

Sift the flour, salt and mustard into a bowl. Rub in the butter until the mixture resembles fine breadcrumbs. Add the grated onion, grated potato, chopped parsley and grated cheese and mix to a fairly stiff dough with the egg and the milk. Knead lightly on a floured surface and roll the scone dough to a circle about 22.5 cm/9 inches in diameter. Divide the scone round into 8 equal sections.

Grease and warm a griddle or heavy-based frying pan. The griddle is hot enough when a piece of the mixture placed on it turns golden-brown underneath in 30 seconds.

Cook the potato and onion cakes for 2 to 3 minutes on each side. Serve hot.
Makes 8

Wholemeal treacle scones

These scones should be served very fresh.

Metric	Imperial
100 g flour	¼ lb flour
100 g wholemeal flour	¼ lb wholemeal flour
25 g sugar	1 oz sugar
1 × 2.5 ml spoon cream of tartar	½ teaspoon cream of tartar
1 × 2.5 ml spoon bicarbonate of soda	½ teaspoon bicarbonate of soda
1 × 5 ml spoon ground mixed spice	1 teaspoon ground mixed spice
50 g butter	2 oz butter
2 × 15 ml spoons black treacle, warmed	2 tablespoons black treacle, warmed
7 × 15 ml spoons milk	7 tablespoons milk

Put the dry ingredients into a bowl and stir until thoroughly mixed. Rub in the butter then stir in the warmed treacle and the 6 × 15 ml spoons/6 tablespoons milk.

Turn the dough out on a floured surface and knead lightly. Roll out gently until about 1 cm/½ inch thick and stamp out about 10 rounds with a 5 cm/2 inch cutter.

Place the scones on a greased and floured baking sheet and brush with remaining milk. Bake in a fairly hot oven (190°C/375°F or Gas Mark 5) for 20 minutes.
Makes 10 to 12

Wholemeal treacle scones

Basic choux pastry

Choux pastry serves equally well as a base for either sweet or savoury dishes. Do remember that baked choux should be stored unfilled, otherwise the pastry starts to soften.

Metric	Imperial
65g plain flour	2½oz plain flour
Pinch of salt	Pinch of salt
50g butter	2oz butter
150ml water	¼ pint water
2 large eggs, lightly beaten	2 large eggs, lightly beaten

Sift the flour and salt together. Put the butter into a saucepan with the water, and bring just to boiling point over a moderate heat, until the butter has melted. Remove the pan from the heat and beat in the sifted flour immediately, until the choux paste forms a smooth ball and leaves the sides of the pan clean. Allow to cool, and then gradually beat in the beaten eggs. If the choux paste is too hot the eggs will curdle.

Eclairs

Put the choux pastry into a piping bag fitted with a 1cm/½inch plain nozzle. Pipe into 10cm/4inch lengths on a greased and floured baking sheet, leaving sufficient space between each one to allow for spreading. The piped choux can easily be removed from the end of the nozzle with a sharp knife. Bake the éclairs in a hot oven (220°C/425°F or Gas Mark 7) for 15 minutes, then reduce the heat to fairly hot (190°C/375°F or Gas Mark 5) for a further 20 minutes. Remove the éclairs to a wire rack and make a slit in the side of each one to allow the steam to escape. Once cold, fill the éclairs with Crème patissière (see opposite page) and coat with coffee, chocolate or vanilla glacé icing.
Makes 10 to 12

Cream buns

Put the choux pastry into a piping bag fitted with a large star nozzle. Pipe small round, raised shapes on to greased and floured baking sheets, leaving space for spreading. Each round of choux should be about 5cm/2 inches in diameter. Bake as for éclairs, and make a small hole in the base of each cooked bun, to allow the steam to escape. Once cold, fill the buns with whipped cream and dust with sifted icing sugar.
Makes 10 to 12

Profiteroles

Put the choux pastry into a piping bag fitted with a 1 cm/½ inch plain nozzle. Pipe very small raised mounds, no more than 2.5 cm/1 inch in diameter, on to greased and floured baking sheets, leaving space for spreading. Bake as for éclairs, but for only 20 minutes, and make a small hole in the base of each cooked profiterole to allow the steam to escape. Once cold, fill with whipped cream. Arrange the profiteroles in a pyramid on a serving dish, and either dust with sifted icing sugar or top with a chocolate sauce.

Serves 4

NOTE: For a party snack the baked profiteroles can be served hot with a savoury filling – try cream cheese flavoured with anchovy essence and mixed with chopped prawns; white sauce mixed with flaked tuna and chopped hard-boiled egg; or minced ham and chutney.

Profiteroles; Eclairs ready for baking; Cream buns

Crème patissière (pastry cream)

This basic custard filling can be flavoured and coloured according to personal taste – grated orange or lemon zest, brandy, almond essence, melted chocolate, or coffee essence can be added, depending on what the pastry cream is to be used for.

Metric	Imperial
2 × 15 ml spoons cornflour	2 tablespoons cornflour
300 ml milk	½ pint milk
1 × 15 ml spoon caster sugar	1 tablespoon caster sugar
Few drops of vanilla essence	Few drops of vanilla essence
2 egg yolks	2 egg yolks
4 × 15 ml spoons whipped cream	4 tablespoons whipped cream

Blend the cornflour with a little of the milk. Put the remaining milk into a saucepan with the sugar and the vanilla essence. Bring the milk to the boil and stir into the blended cornflour. Return the mixture to the saucepan and cook, stirring constantly, until the mixture thickens.

Remove from the heat and beat in the egg yolks. Stir over gentle heat for a few minutes to cook the egg but do not allow to boil. Cover the pastry cream with a circle of dampened greaseproof paper until you are ready to use it, to prevent a skin forming, and cool. Fold in the whipped cream and any chosen additional flavouring or food colouring.

Makes approx. 450 ml/¾ pint

Peanut biscuits

Orange, carrot and nut cake

This cake improves in flavour if kept for at least one day before cutting.

Metric	Imperial
100g butter	¼lb butter
175g caster sugar	6oz caster sugar
1×5ml spoon ground cinnamon	1 teaspoon ground cinnamon
1×5ml spoon grated orange zest	1 teaspoon grated orange zest
2 eggs, lightly beaten	2 eggs, lightly beaten
75g raw carrot, finely grated	3oz raw carrot, finely grated
50g walnuts, finely chopped	2oz walnuts, finely chopped
1×15ml spoon orange juice	1 tablespoon orange juice
225g self-raising flour	½lb self-raising flour
Pinch of salt	Pinch of salt

Cream the butter and sugar together in a bowl until pale and fluffy. Beat in the ground cinnamon and orange zest. Gradually add the eggs, beating well after each addition. Stir in the grated carrot, chopped nuts and orange juice. Sift the flour and salt together and fold into the creamed mixture.

Peanut biscuits

Home-made biscuits and cookies give a surprisingly big yield for the amount of time and trouble involved. This recipe is a little richer than the average biscuit.

Metric	Imperial
275g self-raising flour	10oz self-raising flour
1×2.5ml spoon ground cinnamon	½ teaspoon ground cinnamon
275g margarine	10oz margarine
225g soft brown sugar	½lb soft brown sugar
100g salted peanuts, finely chopped	¼lb salted peanuts, finely chopped
100g seedless raisins	¼lb seedless raisins
1–2×15ml spoons milk	1–2 tablespoons milk

Sift the flour and cinnamon together. Cream the margarine and sugar together until light and fluffy. Fold in the flour with the chopped peanuts and raisins and sufficient milk to make a soft dough.

Using half the mixture, drop teaspoonfuls on to two baking sheets, allowing room to spread. Bake in a moderate oven (180°C/350°F or Gas Mark 4) for 10 minutes. Remove with a palette knife and cool on a wire rack while baking the second batch.

Makes approx. 48

Orange, carrot and nut cake

Turn into a greased 20 cm/8 inch cake tin lined with greased greaseproof paper and smooth the top. Bake in a warm oven 160°C/325°F or Gas Mark 3) for 45 to 55 minutes, or until the centre of the cake springs back when lightly pressed with a fingertip. Turn out on a wire rack to cool. If liked, the cake can be decorated with orange glacé, butter icing, or sifted icing sugar.

Oat crisps

Oat crisps

These thin crispy biscuits just melt in the mouth.

Metric	Imperial
150 g butter	*5 oz butter*
50 g golden syrup	*2 oz golden syrup*
100 g demerara sugar	*¼ lb demerara sugar*
75 g quick cook oats	*3 oz quick cook oats*
50 g desiccated coconut	*2 oz desiccated coconut*
100 g plain flour	*¼ lb plain flour*
1 × 5 ml spoon bicarbonate of soda	*1 teaspoon bicarbonate of soda*
1 × 5 ml spoon hot water	*1 teaspoon hot water*

Place the butter, syrup and sugar in a large saucepan. Heat gently until the butter has melted and the sugar dissolved. Mix together the oats, coconut and flour, then stir into the melted mixture. Dissolve the bicarbonate of soda in the hot water and stir into the oat mixture. Allow to cool for a few minutes then form into 18 balls.

Place the balls well apart on greased baking sheets. Leave plenty of space for spreading. Bake in a warm oven (160°C/325°F or Gas Mark 3) for 15 to 20 minutes, or until evenly browned. Leave to cool slightly and set before removing them with a palette knife. Cool on a wire rack. Store in an airtight container.

Dripping gingerbread

Family sponge

This useful basic cake mixture can be varied to provide layer cakes of different flavours, a light fruit cake, or little cup cakes that are easy to decorate.

Metric	Imperial
175 g butter or margarine	6 oz butter or margarine
175 g sugar	6 oz sugar
3 eggs	3 eggs
225 g self-raising flour	½ lb self-raising flour
Pinch of salt	Pinch of salt
2 × 15 ml spoons milk	2 tablespoons milk
4 × 15 ml spoons jam	4 tablespoons jam
Caster sugar to sprinkle	Caster sugar to sprinkle

Dripping gingerbread

A well-flavoured cake using wholewheat flour and dripping. It is best kept for at least one day before using.

Metric	Imperial
350 g wholewheat flour	¾ lb wholewheat flour
Pinch of salt	Pinch of salt
2 × 5 ml spoons ground ginger	2 teaspoons ground ginger
100 g beef dripping	¼ lb beef dripping
100 g golden syrup	¼ lb golden syrup
100 g black treacle	¼ lb black treacle
75 g soft brown sugar	3 oz soft brown sugar
1 × 5 ml spoon bicarbonate of soda	1 teaspoon bicarbonate of soda
150 ml milk, warmed	¼ pint milk, warmed

Sift the flour, salt and ground ginger together into a large mixing bowl. Melt the dripping, golden syrup, treacle and brown sugar gently in a saucepan over low heat. Add to the flour and beat well. Dissolve the bicarbonate of soda in the warm milk. Add to the beaten mixture and mix thoroughly.

Pour into a greased 25 × 20 cm/10 × 8 inch tin, lined with greased greaseproof paper. Bake in a cool oven (150°C/300°F or Gas Mark 2) for about 1 hour, or until a fine skewer inserted in the centre comes out clean. Leave the gingerbread to cool in the tin, then turn out and strip off the lining paper. Store in an airtight tin to keep the cake moist.

Cream the butter and sugar together until pale and fluffy. Add the eggs one at a time beating well after each addition. Fold in the flour and salt with the milk.

Turn the mixture into a greased 20 cm/8 inch square cake tin lined with greased greaseproof paper. Bake in a moderate oven (180°C/350°F or Gas Mark 4) for 30 to 35 minutes, or until well risen and golden-brown. The cake will have shrunk slightly from the sides of the tin.

Turn the cake out on a wire rack to cool. When cold split into 2 layers and sandwich together with the jam and sprinkle with caster sugar. Serve cut into squares.

Coconut cake

Add 75 g/3 oz desiccated coconut with the flour, spread a little more jam over the top of the finished cake and sprinkle coconut round the edge.

Fruit cake

Add the grated zest of 1 orange to the creamed mixture and 75 g/3 oz mixed dried fruit, (sultanas, raisins, currants) with the flour. Bake for 40 to 45 minutes.

Cup cakes

The mixture may be baked in paper cases in well-greased bun tins for about 15 minutes. Top with glacé icing or brush with melted red currant jelly, sprinkle with coconut and top with half a glacé cherry.

(clockwise) Coconut cake; Cup cakes; Fruit cake; Family sponge

Making more of your leftovers

These days, very little meat is left over from the weekend joint, but far more often there are leftovers from a chicken or turkey meal. Recipes are given here to use these up to make yet another main meal. There are also ideas for using leftover vegetables and these dishes often become so popular that it pays to cook more vegetables than will be required, specially to make them.

The bone from any joint is worth keeping to contribute some goodness to making stock, but there is no doubt that boiling bacon or ham produces at the same time the most flavoursome stock of all. It is necessary to soak some ham and bacon joints to remove excess salt before cooking, or to throw away the first water in which it is brought to the boil. This ensures that the stock will not be too salty to use.

The old-fashioned idea of cooking a joint with vegetables or pulses to provide two separate main meals is more practical today with bacon than with beef, so these recipes include a real country dish, Boiled gammon with pease pudding. This gives you one meal of hot gammon with pease pudding and root vegetables, a rich soup and fried slices of leftover pease pudding for the next day, and even cold gammon for sandwiches.

Bone stock tomato soup

An easily made, well-flavoured soup using ham stock left over from boiling a joint. For special occasions swirl a spoonful of cream in each bowl and top with a little chopped parsley or snipped chives.

Metric	Imperial
25 g butter	*1 oz butter*
½ kg onions, peeled and chopped	*1 lb onions, peeled and chopped*
4 medium-sized carrots, peeled and chopped	*4 medium-sized carrots, peeled and chopped*
2 medium-sized potatoes, peeled and chopped	*2 medium-sized potatoes peeled and chopped*
2 celery stalks, scrubbed and chopped	*2 celery stalks, scrubbed and chopped*
1 clove of garlic, crushed	*1 clove of garlic, crushed*
Pinch of dried basil	*Pinch of dried basil*
2 litres ham stock	*3½ pints ham stock*
1 × 15 ml spoon soft brown sugar	*1 tablespoon soft brown sugar*
1 × 156 g can tomato purée	*1 × 5½ oz can tomato purée*
Salt and freshly ground black pepper	*Salt and freshly ground black pepper*

Melt the butter in a saucepan. Add the chopped vegetables and crushed garlic and stir for 3 to 4 minutes until well coated with the butter. Add the basil and sufficient of the stock to cover the vegetables. Bring to the boil, lower the heat, cover and simmer for 20 minutes, or until the vegetables are tender. Liquidize in an electric blender or press through a sieve.

Return the purée to the rinsed-out pan and add the remaining stock, brown sugar, tomato purée and seasoning to taste. Bring the soup back to the boil and simmer for 20 to 30 minutes. Check the seasoning and serve hot.

Bone stock tomato soup

Turkey plait

Casserole curry

Turkey plait

A savoury filling, encased in puff pastry, which makes a meal from a small amount of leftover turkey meat.

Metric	Imperial
25 g butter	1 oz butter
1 onion, peeled and sliced	1 onion, peeled and sliced
75 g button mushrooms, wiped and sliced	3 oz button mushrooms, wiped and sliced
¼ kg cooked turkey, boned and diced	½ lb cooked turkey, boned and diced
175 g Gouda cheese, grated	6 oz Gouda cheese, grated
1 small red pepper, deseeded and sliced	1 small red pepper, deseeded and sliced
1 × 2.5 ml spoon dried mixed herbs	½ level teaspoon dried mixed herbs
Salt and freshly ground black pepper	Salt and freshly ground black pepper
1 egg, beaten	1 egg, beaten
225 g frozen puff pastry, defrosted	½ lb frozen puff pastry, defrosted

Melt the butter in a saucepan and cook the sliced onion and mushrooms over moderate heat for 5 minutes, stirring occasionally. Stir in the diced turkey, grated cheese, sliced red pepper and mixed herbs. Season to taste and stir in most of the beaten egg, reserving a little for glazing.

Roll out the pastry to an oblong 34 × 30 cm / 14 × 12 inches. Spoon the filling down the middle of the pastry, leaving a wide margin all round. Using a sharp knife cut parallel slits about 1 cm / ½ inch wide, down each side of the oblong. Fold up the top and bottom of the oblong on to the filling. Plait the strips over the filling. Transfer on to a damp baking sheet.

Brush the turkey plait with the remainder of the beaten egg. Cook for 20 minutes in a hot oven (220°C/425°F or Gas Mark 7) and then reduce heat to fairly hot (190°C/375°F) or Gas Mark 5 for a further 10 minutes.

Serve hot or cold with a green salad.

Casserole curry

An optional extra with this dish would be poppadums, which can be bought ready-made and only need to be fried for 30 seconds on each side in a little hot vegetable oil. Drain them on absorbent kitchen paper.

Metric	Imperial
1 × 15 ml spoon corn oil	1 tablespoon corn oil
1 large onion, peeled and finely chopped	1 large onion, peeled and finely chopped
2 × 15 ml spoons curry powder	2 tablespoons curry powder
1 × 15 ml spoon cornflour	1 tablespoon cornflour
900 ml chicken stock	1½ pints chicken stock
1 medium-sized cooking apple, peeled, cored and grated	1 medium-sized cooking apple, peeled, cored and grated
1 × 15 ml spoon apricot jam	1 tablespoon apricot jam
2 × 15 ml spoons desiccated coconut	2 tablespoons desiccated coconut
2 × 5 ml spoons lemon juice	2 teaspoons lemon juice
Salt to taste	Salt to taste
350 g cooked chicken or turkey, diced	¾ lb cooked chicken or turkey, diced
25 g seedless raisins	1 oz seedless raisins

Heat the corn oil in a saucepan and cook the chopped onion in it for a few minutes until limp and transparent. Add the curry powder and the cornflour and cook over low heat for a further 3 minutes. Stir in the stock, grated apple, apricot jam and coconut. Simmer for a further 30 minutes, stirring occasionally.

Add the lemon juice and adjust seasoning if necessary. Stir in the diced chicken or turkey and the raisins and reheat to make the dish piping hot.

Serve in the traditional way with boiled long-grain rice and chutney.

Boiled gammon with pease pudding

Boiled gammon with pease pudding

This recipe provides a nourishing and substantial meal for one wintry day and a filling soup for the next. There should also be sufficient cold gammon to make sandwiches as well.

A pressure cooker may be used to advantage. Cook the gammon piece for 30 minutes at high pressure. When adding the vegetables for the first meal, bring to high pressure and cook for 5 minutes.

Metric	Imperial
½ kg yellow split peas, washed, covered with hot water and soaked overnight	1 lb yellow split peas, washed, covered with hot water and soaked overnight
1 corner gammon joint (about 1½ kg), soaked in cold water overnight	1 corner gammon joint (about 3 lb), soaked in cold water overnight
1 bouquet garni	1 bouquet garni
Salt and freshly ground black pepper	Salt and freshly ground black pepper
50 g butter	2 oz butter

VEGETABLES FOR THE SOUP:

4 medium-sized carrots, peeled and chopped	4 medium-sized carrots, peeled and chopped
4 medium-sized onions, peeled and chopped	4 medium-sized onions, peeled and chopped
4 leeks, white and pale green part washed, trimmed and chopped	4 leeks, white and pale green part washed, trimmed and chopped
6 large celery stalks, scrubbed and chopped	6 large celery stalks, scrubbed and chopped

VEGETABLES FOR THE FIRST MEAL:

4 medium-sized carrots, peeled and quartered	4 medium-sized carrots, peeled and quartered
4 medium-sized onions, peeled and quartered	4 medium-sized onions, peeled and quartered
4 leeks, white and pale green part washed and halved	4 leeks, white and pale green part washed and halved
1 small swede, peeled and cut into large chunks	1 small swede, peeled and cut into large chunks

Drain the split peas, rinse under cold running water and tie all but a handful in a scalded muslin cloth. Drain the gammon and place in a large saucepan with the bouquet garni, loose and tied peas, seasoning and soup vegetables. Cover with about 2 litres / 3½ pints cold water and bring to the boil, skimming with a slotted draining spoon. Lower the heat and simmer gently for about 1½ hours (allowing 25 to 30 minutes per ½ kg / 1 lb) or until the gammon is tender. Taste the soup and adjust the seasoning if necessary.

Remove the gammon from the pan, strip off the rind and keep the joint hot. Turn the peas from the muslin into a serving dish. Add the butter and beat with a fork until smooth. Taste and adjust the seasoning, if necessary, and keep hot. Meanwhile add the vegetables for the first meal to the saucepan. Bring back to the boil and simmer for 15 minutes or until tender.

Remove the vegetables for the first meal carefully with a slotted draining spoon. Serve with the gammon, pease pudding, English mustard and, if desired, plain boiled potatoes or wholemeal bread. Any remaining pease pudding may be blended into the soup to be served the following day or fried gently in a little butter and served with bacon.

NOTE: In the interest of economy, this dish may be prepared with a gammon shank or forehock.

Farmer's style noodles

This is an excellent dish for using up leftovers from a roast chicken.

Metric	Imperial
2 × 15 ml spoons vegetable oil	2 tablespoons vegetable oil
1 large onion, peeled and finely chopped	1 large onion, peeled and finely chopped
100 g button mushrooms, wiped and chopped	¼ lb button mushrooms, wiped and chopped
1 × 396 g can tomatoes	1 × 14 oz can tomatoes
1 × 15 ml spoon tomato purée	1 tablespoon tomato purée
1 clove of garlic, crushed	1 clove of garlic, crushed
1 × 5 ml spoon dried rosemary	1 teaspoon dried rosemary
Salt and freshly ground black pepper	Salt and freshly ground black pepper
100 g cooked boned chicken, or other meat, chopped	¼ lb cooked boned chicken, or other meat, chopped
100 g ham, chopped	¼ lb ham, chopped
350 g noodles	¾ lb noodles

Heat the oil in a saucepan. Add the chopped onion and fry gently for 5 minutes. Add the chopped mushrooms and cook for a further few minutes. Add the canned tomatoes and their juice, tomato purée, crushed garlic, rosemary, and seasoning to taste. Bring to the boil and simmer for 20 minutes. Add the chopped chicken and ham and reheat.

Meanwhile, cook the noodles in a pan of rapidly boiling salted water. Drain the noodles thoroughly, place on a serving dish and spoon over the chicken and ham sauce. For easy eating serve in deep soup bowls.

Farmer's style noodles

Layered casserole; Mashed potato cakes; Peasant's omelette

Ideas for dishes using leftover vegetables

Layered casserole
Grease a small casserole, fill with layers of chopped, mixed cooked vegetables, fresh sliced apple and diced cooked bacon. Cover with cheese sauce and bake for 25 minutes in a fairly hot oven (190°C/375°F or Gas Mark 5)

Mashed potato cakes
Mix together equal quantities of leftover mashed potato and minced cooked meat. Season with chopped parsley, grated onion, salt and freshly ground black pepper to taste. Shape into round cakes, coat in seasoned flour and fry in dripping until golden-brown on both sides. Serve with tomato slices.

Peasant's omelette
Dice cooked potato and add 2 × 15 ml spoons / 2 tablespoons of it to each two-egg omelette, together with a little grated apple, onion, dried mixed herbs and grated nutmeg. Fry the omelette in leftover bacon fat if possible, or in butter, until the surface is just set.

The elegant extras

A meal starter is sometimes looked upon as an unnecessary extravagance. If made at home it need cost very little, and not only does it add a touch of elegance to any menu but partially satisfies appetites before the main course.

Mousses and creams, especially those made with smoked fish, are tasty starters and the most popular alternative is a good pâté. Either look very attractive served with a small salad garnish, and fresh hot toast.

Avocado pears are deservedly fashionable and popular but the cost is often prohibitive. Here you will find four suggestions for combining one avocado with other ingredients to serve four people as a starter.

Kipper mousse

This is a light mousse with a piquant flavour which is easy to turn out and is ideal served as a starter or with a salad.

Metric	Imperial
225 g kipper fillets	½ lb kipper fillets
150 ml chicken stock	¼ pint chicken stock
15 g gelatine	½ oz gelatine
4 × 5 ml spoons lemon juice	4 teaspoons lemon juice
75 g butter, melted	3 oz butter, melted
75 g Gouda cheese, grated	3 oz Gouda cheese, grated
Freshly ground black pepper	Freshly ground black pepper
Lemon and cucumber slices to garnish	Lemon and cucumber slices to garnish

Grill the kippers, or cook boil-in-the-bag kipper in boiling water. Skin and flake. Place the stock and gelatine in a pan and heat to dissolve the gelatine. Liquidize all the ingredients in a blender.

Pour into a rinsed mould or dish to set. To unmould, dip the dish in hot water and invert on to a plate. Garnish with lemon and cucumber slices.

Can be served as a spread on biscuits or with toast.

Kipper mousse; Stuffed lemons

Stuffed lemons

A most effective start to a meal which is also economical when lemons are abundant.

Metric	Imperial
6 fresh lemons	6 fresh lemons
1 × 124 g can sardines in oil, or tuna fish, drained	1 × 4⅜ oz can sardines in oil, or tuna fish, drained
Pinch of paprika	Pinch of paprika
Freshly ground black pepper	Freshly ground black pepper
1 × 5 ml spoon French mustard	1 teaspoon French mustard
6 × 15 ml spoons mayonnaise	6 tablespoons mayonnaise
1 egg white, stiffly beaten	1 egg white, stiffly beaten
TO FINISH:	TO FINISH:
Shredded lettuce	Shredded lettuce
Parsley sprigs	Parsley sprigs

Cut the tops off the lemons. Cut a thin slice off the bottom of the lemons carefully, so that they will stand firmly. Ease out the flesh with a knife and teaspoon. Discard the pith, pips and membranes and chop the flesh.

Place the fish in a basin and mash to a smooth paste. Season with the paprika, black pepper and mustard. Stir in the lemon flesh and the mayonnaise. Sharpen to taste with a little of the lemon juice. Fold in the stiffly beaten egg white. Taste and adjust the seasoning if necessary.

Stuff the lemons with the fish mixture, mounding up at the tops. Chill in the refrigerator. Serve in egg cups or small dishes surrounded by shredded lettuce. Decorate with a sprig of parsley.
Makes 6

Avocado starters

Half an avocado is a perfect way to start a meal, but there are many different ways of using this 'vegetable pear', rather than filling its centre with French dressing. And, you don't have to serve half an avocado per person. Here are just a few unusual ideas for economical, quick-to-prepare avocado starters, each one serving 4.

(clockwise from left) Taramavocado; Avocado and cheese croûtes; Avocado Maryland; Italian starter

Avocado and cheese croûtes

Spread 4 slices of rye bread with butter and a little French mustard. Halve 1 avocado pear, and remove the stone and peel. Cut the avocado into slices and arrange on top of the rye bread. Sprinkle each slice with a generous topping of grated cheese and pop under the grill until bubbling and golden.

Taramavocado

Halve 1 avocado pear, and remove the stone. Scoop the flesh into a bowl with a teaspoon. Add the juice and grated zest of half a lemon, 75 g / 3 oz smoked cod's roe, 1 crushed clove of garlic, and salt and freshly ground black pepper to taste. Pound to a smooth creamy paste. Stir in 3 × 15 ml spoons / 3 tablespoons whipped cream. Spoon into small cocotte dishes and garnish with black olives.

Italian starter

Crumble 100 g / ¼ lb Dolcelatte cheese. Halve 1 avocado pear, and remove the stone and peel. Cut the avocado into thin slices and toss lightly in French dressing. Arrange the cheese and avocado on a bed of lettuce and spoon over a little extra French dressing.

Avocado Maryland

Halve 1 avocado pear and remove the stone. Scoop the flesh into a bowl with a teaspoon. Add the juice and grated zest of half a lemon, 100 g / ¼ lb chopped cooked chicken, and salt and freshly ground black pepper to taste. Beat until well combined and stir in 2 × 15 ml spoons / 2 tablespoons drained sweetcorn and 2 × 15 ml spoons / 2 tablespoons single cream. Spoon into small dishes and sprinkle with crisply grilled and chopped bacon.

129

Fruit starters

Citrus fruits, such as oranges and grapefruit, make a refreshing base for many quick-to-prepare starters, and their characteristic sharp flavour contrasts so well with many richer ingredients. Here are just three ideas for hors d'oeuvre based on fruit.

Orange, cottage cheese and ham salad

Here is an elegant meal starter, well worth the effort of making if the main dish is not too substantial.

Metric	Imperial
2 oranges	2 oranges
¼ kg cottage cheese	½ lb cottage cheese
¼ kg cooked ham, or other cooked meat, chopped	¼ lb cooked ham, or other cooked meat, chopped
1 onion, peeled and grated	1 onion, peeled and grated
Salt and freshly ground black pepper	Salt and freshly ground black pepper
25 g preserved stem ginger, chopped	1 oz preserved stem ginger, chopped
Sprigs of watercress to garnish	Sprigs of watercress to garnish

Orange, grapefruit and date salad

Finely grate the zest from 1 orange. Remove all the peel and pith from both oranges. Cutting between each section membrane, remove the segments from the oranges, discarding the pips.

Mix the cottage cheese with the grated orange zest, chopped ham, grated onion, salt and pepper to taste, and the chopped ginger.

Spoon the salad into the centres of 4 small dishes or plates, and arrange the orange segments and sprigs of watercress around the edges. Serve with slices of pumpernickel.

Orange, cottage cheese and ham salad

Orange, grapefruit and date salad

The flavour of this salad starter resembles the Italian delicacy, Mostarda di frutta – a variety of fruits preserved in a mustard-flavoured syrup. This dish can equally well be served as a dessert, if the mustard and seasoning are omitted.

Metric	Imperial
2 oranges	2 oranges
1 grapefruit	1 grapefruit
8 fresh dates, stoned and chopped	8 fresh dates, stoned and chopped
3 × 15 ml spoons clear honey	3 tablespoons clear honey
3 × 5 ml spoons French mustard	3 teaspoons French mustard
2 × 15 ml spoons lemon juice	2 tablespoons lemon juice
Salt and freshly ground black pepper	Salt and freshly ground black pepper

Remove all the peel and pith from the oranges and the grapefruit. Cut the fruits into thin slices, and cut each slice into 3 or 4 sections.

Mix together the orange and grapefruit pieces in a bowl with the chopped fresh dates. Combine the honey, French mustard, lemon juice and seasoning to taste.

Spoon the mustard and honey dressing over the prepared fruit and toss lightly. Chill for at least 1 hour.

Spoon the salad out on 4 small dishes, and serve with sliced salami, or other Continental sausage.

Orange, chicken and bean sprout salad

An excellent dish for using up leftovers from a roast chicken.

Metric	Imperial
175 g cooked, boned chicken	6 oz cooked, boned chicken
2 oranges	2 oranges
175 g fresh bean sprouts	6 oz fresh bean sprouts
FOR THE DRESSING:	FOR THE DRESSING:
4 × 15 ml spoons orange juice	4 tablespoons orange juice
2 × 15 ml spoons lemon juice	2 tablespoons lemon juice
150 ml olive or corn oil	¼ pint olive or corn oil
Salt and freshly ground black pepper	Salt and freshly ground black pepper
TO GARNISH:	TO GARNISH:
2 × 15 ml spoons chopped parsley	2 tablespoons chopped parsley
25 g cashew nuts, chopped	1 oz cashew nuts, chopped

Remove any skin from the chicken meat and pull it into shreds. (This is more easily done while the chicken is still warm, and it is best to take any leftovers from the carcase of a chicken as soon after cooking as possible.)

Remove all the peel and white pith from the oranges. Cutting between each section membrane, remove the segments from the oranges, discarding the pips. Put the orange segments into a bowl with the bean sprouts and chicken. To make the dressing, put the orange and lemon juices into a screw topped jar with the oil and seasoning to taste. Shake vigorously.

Pour the dressing over the chicken, orange segments and bean sprouts, and toss lightly together. Spoon the salad out on 4 small dishes or plates, and sprinkle with chopped parsley and cashew nuts.

Orange, chicken and bean sprout salad

Slimming on a slender budget

Many would-be slimmers are deterred when they glance through a diet sheet, and see how expensive the diet would be to follow. Lean meat for grilling is high in protein but relatively high in cost, and it is frequently called for by most slimming plans. Also, it may be difficult to stick to the plan when you have to cook for other members of the family and eat with them. Nobody likes to be teased about a serious effort to lose weight, and the less obvious it is that you are dieting at all, the more likely you are to carry on and achieve a satisfactory weight loss in the end.

Our busy lives make a starvation regime undesirable, and most doctors frown on 'crash' diets, which bring dramatic but short-lived results. Therefore, a healthy, satisfying diet has been designed, based on a sufficient supply of high protein food other than meat. It probably costs no more than you would usually spend on food. And it really gets results.

The simple fare diet

This diet allows good, fresh, health-giving food in plenty; food like cheese, tomatoes, mushrooms, green vegetables and fruit, full of vitamins and essential nutrients. The cheese suggested is Edam, because it is the hard cheese lowest in calories. The diet is carefully balanced to provide about 1,200 calories every day. If you follow it carefully, you should lose 1 kg/2 lb a week, or perhaps a little more. For times when you feel you need them, a few extra nibbles and treats are listed. Start off by having some nibbles every day, and then if you find you are not losing weight fast enough, cut them out. Not only will your weight diminish, but with all this fresh food each day, your hair, skin and general appearance will benefit too.

Instead of feeling deprived and bored, on the Simple Fare Diet, you will feel energetic, and as fit as if you had just come back from a sunny holiday. To achieve the best results, follow the diet for a fortnight. You can always return to the diet again, even for one week. As it includes suggestions for seven breakfasts, seven light meals and seven main meals, you can ring the changes, and never be forced to repeat even one meal throughout a week.

What to do

The programme is straightforward and simple. Memorize the following points, or keep a copy of the basic rules handy for reference.

Every day choose one of the seven breakfasts, seven light meals and seven main meals that are set out below, plus any vegetables from your 'vegetable nibble bowl' and one of the special nibble treats.

You are allowed 600 ml/1 pint of milk a day, for use in tea and coffee and where mentioned in the recipes. (It might be a good idea to separate your own bottle of milk from your family's supply every morning so that you can see at a glance how much you've had, and how much you've got left, throughout the day.)

There is no need to limit intake of low-calorie liquids, such as water, meat extract drinks and low-calorie squashes. Tea and coffee are also unlimited as long as you only use milk from your allowance and artificial sweeteners. (But try to do without too much of either drink.)

A list of fruits for the fruit portions mentioned are given here together with a list of nibbles allowed and some family-style recipes.

So you see your menu can vary every day, but at the same time you can be sure you are getting a nutritionally sound, carefully controlled calorie intake. And you will not be complaining of hunger pangs. Fresh vegetables and generous helpings of cheese are as satisfying as they are nutritious!

Breakfasts

Choose from one of the following:

1. 1 portion fresh fruit (see list)
   50 g/2 oz grilled kidney with 50 g/2 oz mushrooms cooked in 1 × 15 ml spoon/1 tablespoon water
   1 rusk (without butter)
   Tea or coffee

2. 25 g/1 oz breakfast cereal with milk from allowance
   Creamed mushrooms. Cook 100 g/¼ lb mushrooms in 2 × 15 ml spoons/2 tablespoons water, remove from heat and stir in 75 ml/3 fl oz unsweetened natural yogurt, salt, pepper and a dash of Worcestershire sauce. Serve on 1 thin slice of toast.

3. 1 small glass fresh orange juice (100 ml/4 fl oz)
   2 rashers streaky bacon, crisply grilled, and 1 sliced tomato on 1 thin slice unbuttered toast
   Tea or coffee

4. Breakfast pizza. Toast 1 thin slice bread and cover with 25 g/1 oz sliced mushrooms, 1 sliced tomato and 25 g/1 oz thinly sliced Edam cheese. Place under a hot grill until the cheese begins to melt.
   Serve garnished with a black olive or pickled walnut
   Portion fresh fruit
   Tea or coffee

5. ½ ripe grapefruit (without sugar)
   1 egg scrambled with 2 × 15 ml spoons/2 tablespoons milk from allowance
   thin slice toast, lightly buttered
   Tea or coffee

Breakfasts 1 to 5

133

Breakfast 6; Breakfast 7

6. ½ ripe grapefruit (without sugar)
   1 boiled egg
   1 thin slice toast, lightly buttered
   Tea or coffee with milk from allowance
7. 1 small glass tomato juice (100 ml / 4 fl oz)
   1 rasher back bacon fried in its own fat with 50 g / 2 oz mushrooms
   1 thin slice toast, lightly buttered
   Tea or coffee

Light meals

1. Savoury baked eggs. Mix together 50 g / 2 oz sliced mushrooms, 2 × 15 ml spoons / 2 tablespoons evaporated milk, salt and pepper. Put in a small ovenproof dish. Break an egg on top and sprinkle with 15 g / ½ oz grated Edam cheese. Bake in a moderate oven (180°C / 350°F or Gas Mark 4) for approximately 15 minutes – until the egg is set and cheese melted.
   Mixed green salad vegetables (no dressing)
   2 rye crispbreads, very lightly buttered
   1 small glass tomato juice (100 ml / 4 fl oz)
2. Tomato cauliflower cheese. Cover a large portion boiled cauliflower with a tomato sauce prepared from 5 × 15 ml spoons / 5 tablespoons condensed cream of tomato soup and a dash of Worcestershire sauce. Sprinkle over the top 25 g / 1 oz grated Edam cheese. Heat under a hot grill until cheese melts.
   1 rye crispbread, unbuttered
   Portion fresh fruit
3. Mushroom omelette. Made from 15 g / ½ oz butter, 2 eggs, 50 g / 2 oz sliced mushrooms, garnished with sprigs of watercress.
   Tea, coffee, yeast or meat extract drink

4. Toasted cheese and pineapple sandwich. Toast 2 thin slices of bread on one side only. Mix together 25 g / 1 oz grated Edam cheese and 1 × 15 ml spoon / 1 tablespoon drained, crushed pineapple and sandwich between toasted sides of bread and toast on the outside. Serve hot.
   Watercress
   Portion fresh fruit
5. Cheese coleslaw. Prepare a dressing from 1 × 15 ml spoon / 1 tablespoon unsweetened natural yogurt, little vinegar, pinch each salt, pepper and sugar. Mix together 50 g / 2 oz shredded white cabbage, ½ small, red eating apple, cored and diced and tossed in 2 × 5 ml spoons / 2 teaspoons lemon juice, 1 × 15 ml spoon / 1 tablespoon grated onion, 50 g / 2 oz diced Edam cheese. Add the dressing and toss well together.
   Serve garnished with parsley, chicory or watercress.
   Portion fresh fruit
6. Mushroom and ham cocotte. Beat together 1 egg, 4 × 15 ml / 4 tablespoons milk from allowance and salt and pepper to taste. Stir in 25 g / 1 oz sliced mushrooms, 25 g / 1 oz chopped lean cooked ham and a little freshly chopped parsley. Pour into a lightly greased individual ovenproof dish and bake in a warm oven (160°C / 325°F or Gas Mark 3) for 20 minutes or until set. Garnish with fresh parsley and serve with green salad vegetables.
   1 small slice bread, lightly buttered
   Portion fresh fruit
7. Sardines au gratin. Toast 1 slice wholemeal bread on 1 side. Place 2 sardines in tomato sauce on untoasted side, sprinkle with lemon juice, a little grated onion and a little chopped parsley. Cover with 25 g / 1 oz grated Edam cheese. Melt under a hot grill. Serve hot.
   Portion fresh fruit

Between-meal nibbles

A 'vegetable nibble bowl' is intended for use whenever the hunger pangs strike – keep it handy in the refrigerator. Have prepared in the bowl some of the following: slices of cucumber, tomato, celery, whole radishes, raw button mushrooms, rings of green pepper and carrot sticks.

Between-meal nibbles

Light meals (right)

Liver casserole

Main meals

Choose from one of the following. Recipes marked ★ are given in full.

1. 1 portion of ★Mushroom and Edam cheese roast with tomato sauce
   Mixed salad from lettuce, chicory, cucumber, watercress, pepper and tomatoes (no dressing)
   175 g/6 oz portion ripe melon (without sugar)
2. Liver casserole. Prepared from 175 g/6 oz lambs' liver, 50 g/2 oz sliced onion, 50 g/2 oz sliced mushrooms and 100 g/¼ lb canned tomatoes with a pinch of dried mixed herbs and seasoning.
   100 g/¼ lb boiled celery and 75 g/3 oz Brussels sprouts or other leafy green vegetables
   25 g/1 oz Edam cheese and 1 rye crispbread
3. Baked chicken joint with mushrooms. Sprinkle a medium-sized chicken joint and 50 g/2 oz button mushrooms with lemon juice and salt and pepper. Wrap in foil. Bake in a fairly hot oven (190°C/375°F, or Gas Mark 5) for 40 minutes.
   75 g/3 oz carrots and 100 g/¼ lb broccoli or other leafy green vegetable
   25 g/1 oz Edam cheese and 2 cream crackers
4. 1 portion ★Cheesy yogurt topped fish
   2 oven baked tomatoes and 100 g/¼ lb green beans
   Portion fresh fruit
5. 1 portion ★Courgette Neapolitan with 1 rasher crisply grilled back bacon
   Portion fresh fruit
6. 1 portion ★Minced beef and aubergine fiesta
   Mixed green salad (without dressing)
   50 g/2 oz vanilla ice cream or 1 medium-sized banana
7. 1 portion ★Patio salad
   Portion fresh fruit

Fresh fruit portions

Medium-sized eating apple
Small (100 g/¼ lb) orange
100 g/¼ lb fresh whole peaches
175 g/6 oz fresh whole apricots
100 g/¼ lb fresh whole cherries
100 g/¼ lb dessert gooseberries
175 g/6 oz grapefruit, peeled
Medium-sized pear
75 g/3 oz fresh pineapple
175 g/6 oz raspberries
175 g/6 oz strawberries
100 g/¼ lb tangerines or satsumas, peeled

Baked chicken joint with mushrooms

Daily treats

Choose from these, one only each day, either at the time of day when you reach your lowest ebb or at the end of the day:
1 small 'fun size' chocolate-coated candy bar *or* 25 g/1 oz wine gums *or* assorted fruit drops *or* Liquorice Allsorts *or* 12 Twiglets *or* 4 cheese crispies *or* 3 cheese crispbreads *or* 3 Nice biscuits *or* 3 Rich Tea fingers *or* 1 milk chocolate digestive biscuit *or* 150 ml/¼ pint of thick soup *or* 150 ml/¼ pint unsweetened natural yogurt *or* small sherry glass of medium sherry *or* 1 measure of gin or whisky with low calorie tonic, bitter lemon or ginger ale.

Mushroom and Edam cheese roast

Cheesy yogurt topped fish

Mushroom and Edam cheese roast

Metric	Imperial
1 large onion, peeled and chopped	1 large onion, peeled and chopped
1 large green pepper deseeded and chopped	1 large green pepper, deseeded and chopped
25 g butter	1 oz butter
175 g mushrooms, sliced	6 oz mushrooms, sliced
100 g fresh brown breadcrumbs	¼ lb fresh brown breadcrumbs
3 eggs, beaten	3 eggs, beaten
Salt and freshly ground black pepper	Salt and freshly ground black pepper
175 g Edam cheese, grated	6 oz Edam cheese, grated
Pinch of dried mixed herbs	Pinch of dried mixed herbs

Gently fry the chopped onion and green pepper together in the butter until soft but not browned. Add the sliced mushrooms and cook for a further 2 minutes. Remove from the heat and add the remaining ingredients, except the cheese and mixed herbs. Mix thoroughly. Grease a 1 kg/2 lb loaf tin and press the mixture into it. Sprinkle over the grated cheese and mixed herbs. Bake in a moderate oven (180°C/350°F, or Gas Mark 4) for 45 minutes. Serve hot with tomato slices, watercress and tomato sauce.

Serves 4

Tomato sauce

Place in a liquidizer or finely chop together a 396 g/14 oz can tomatoes, ½ small peeled onion, salt and pepper to taste and a dash of Worcestershire sauce. Heat in a pan for 5 minutes before serving.

Serves 4

Cheesy yogurt topped fish

Metric	Imperial
¾ kg fresh or frozen cod or haddock fillets, defrosted	1½ lb fresh or frozen cod or haddock fillets, defrosted
300 ml unsweetened natural yogurt	½ pint unsweetened natural yogurt
1 × 5 ml spoon dry mustard	1 teaspoon dry mustard
Freshly ground black pepper	Freshly ground black pepper
175 g Edam cheese, grated	6 oz Edam cheese, grated
Parsley sprigs to garnish	Parsley sprigs to garnish

Place the fish in a lightly greased shallow baking dish. Mix together the yogurt, mustard, pepper and 100 g/¼ lb of the cheese. Spread over the fish. Bake in a moderate oven (180°C/350°F or Gas Mark 4) for 20 to 25 minutes. Sprinkle with the remaining grated cheese. Return to the oven for about 10 minutes until cheese melts. Garnish with sprigs of parsley.

Serves 4

Courgette Neapolitan

Metric	Imperial
½ kg fresh tomatoes, skinned, or 396 g can tomatoes	1 lb fresh tomatoes, skinned, or 14 oz can tomatoes
1 small onion, peeled and chopped	1 small onion, peeled and chopped
Salt and freshly ground black pepper	Salt and freshly ground black pepper
¾ kg courgettes	1½ lb courgettes
2 × 15 ml spoons flour	2 tablespoons flour
25 g butter	1 oz butter
225 g Edam cheese, thinly sliced	½ lb Edam cheese, thinly sliced

Chop the tomatoes and heat in a saucepan with the chopped onion and seasoning to taste, for 10 minutes, to make a thick tomato sauce. Slice the courgettes into 1 cm / ½ inch rings and then into quarters. Shake in a bag with the flour to coat evenly. Melt the butter in a large frying pan and fry the courgettes until brown on both sides. Put alternate layers of courgette, the tomato mixture and the cheese in a shallow baking dish, finishing with a layer of cheese. Bake in a fairly hot oven (190°C/375°F or Gas Mark 5) for 30 minutes. Serve topped with grilled bacon

Serves 4

Courgette Neapolitan

Minced beef and aubergine fiesta

Minced beef and aubergine fiesta

Metric	Imperial
½ kg lean minced beef	1 lb lean minced beef
1 large onion, peeled and chopped	1 large onion, peeled and chopped
Salt and freshly ground black pepper	Salt and freshly ground black pepper
½ kg aubergines	1 lb aubergines
Boiling water	Boiling water
1 × 396 g can tomatoes, drained	1 × 14 oz can tomatoes, drained
¼ kg mushrooms, sliced	½ lb mushrooms, sliced
1 clove of garlic, crushed	1 clove of garlic, crushed
1 × 1.25 ml spoon salt	¼ teaspoon salt
100 g Edam cheese, grated	¼ lb Edam cheese, grated
Chopped parsley to garnish	Chopped parsley to garnish

Patio salad

Metric	Imperial
50 g canned tuna	2 oz canned tuna
50 g Edam cheese, diced	2 oz Edam cheese, diced
50 g button mushrooms, wiped and cut in quarters	2 oz button mushrooms, wiped and cut in quarters
1 large stalk celery, scrubbed and chopped	1 large stalk celery, scrubbed and chopped
25 g black olives	1 oz black olives
Few lettuce leaves, shredded, to finish	Few lettuce leaves, shredded, to finish
FOR THE DRESSING:	FOR THE DRESSING:
Pinch each of salt, pepper and sugar	Pinch each of salt, pepper and sugar
Good pinch of dry mustard	Good pinch of dry mustard
2 × 5 ml spoons vinegar	2 teaspoons vinegar
1 × 15 ml spoon salad oil	1 tablespoon salad oil

Prepare the dressing by shaking together the seasonings, vinegar and oil. Drain the oil from the fish and break into chunks. Place this and all the other ingredients, except the lettuce leaves, in a bowl. Pour over the dressing and mix well. Allow to stand for at least 30 minutes in a cold place. Serve on a bed of shredded lettuce.
Serves 2

Patio salad

Fry the minced beef in a pan in its own fat until it is browned. Remove from the pan with a slotted draining spoon, leaving the fat behind. Fry the chopped onion in the fat until soft but not browned. Add to the minced beef with seasoning to taste. Place the beef mixture in a lightly greased ovenproof dish.

Peel the aubergines, cut into 2.5 cm / 1 inch slices and cut each slice into 4 triangular pieces. Put in a saucepan, cover with boiling water and cook for 10 minutes. Drain well. Roughly chop the tomatoes and mix with the aubergines, sliced mushrooms, crushed garlic and 1 × 1.25 ml spoon / ¼ teaspoon salt. Spread over the minced beef. Bake uncovered in a fairly hot oven (200°C/400°F or Gas Mark 6) for about 20 minutes. Sprinkle over the grated cheese and bake for a further 10 minutes, until the cheese has melted. Garnish with chopped parsley.
Serves 4

Parties that sparkle

Informal parties are frequently given to save the trouble of setting a table for large numbers. Yet a supper party seems to lack something if there is not one hot main dish included. Two suggestions are given here, the one for twelve people being specially suitable for teenagers with hearty appetites. You may find it useful to have as reference dinner party menus which entail only a reasonable amount of work and yet provide a pleasant, well-balanced selection of food. It is a realistic economy in time to offer a first course which requires only simple preparation, such as buttered corn-on-the-cob.

Cocktail party nibbles can easily come straight from packs, but you will earn extra praise as a hostess if you make some of your own. Stuffed fresh dates are quick to prepare and add a luxury touch.

Catering on a budget for small children is not as easy as it once was. A breakfast cereal crust with a creamy filling cuts up into easily handled wedges and makes just the kind of pie children most enjoy.

Recipes marked * can be found elsewhere in the book.

Dinner party for four

Menu

Smoked mackerel with hot toast

Partridges in piquant sauce

*Turnip and potato purée

*Sweet winter salad

Oranges che yang

Crème Chantilly

Partridges in piquant sauce

This is an elegant yet inexpensive dish when feathered game is in season. The same recipe can equally well be used with pigeons.

Metric	Imperial
4 small partridges, plucked and drawn	4 small partridges, plucked and drawn
50 g lard	2 oz lard
3 medium-sized onions, peeled and sliced	3 medium-sized onions, peeled and sliced
2 stalks of celery, scrubbed and chopped	2 stalks of celery, scrubbed and chopped
1 cooking apple, peeled, cored and roughly chopped	1 cooking apple, peeled, cored and roughly chopped
2 × 15 ml spoons flour	2 tablespoons flour
300 ml chicken stock	½ pint chicken stock
2 × 15 ml spoons Worcestershire sauce	2 tablespoons Worcestershire sauce
50 g seedless raisins	2 oz seedless raisins
Salt and freshly ground black pepper	Salt and freshly ground black pepper
150 ml unsweetened natural yogurt	¼ pint unsweetened natural yogurt
Pastry fleurons to finish	Pastry fleurons to finish

Wash the partridges and dry well with absorbent kitchen paper. Melt the lard in a heavy pan and lightly brown the partridges on all sides. Remove them from the pan and place in a casserole. Cook the onion gently in the remaining fat in the pan for 5 minutes or until limp, then add the chopped celery and the apple. Stir in the flour and cook for another 2 minutes. Gradually add the stock and the Worcestershire sauce, bring to the boil and add the raisins. Add seasoning to taste.

Pour the sauce over the partridges, cover lightly with foil and cook in a moderate oven (180°C/350°F or Gas Mark 4) for 1½ hours, or until the partridges are tender. Remove them and place on a warm serving dish together with the onions, apples and raisins strained from the sauce. Taste the sauce, and adjust the seasoning if necessary. Stir in the yogurt and reheat without boiling. Pour a little of the sauce over the partridges, surround them with the fleurons and serve the rest of the sauce separately in a sauceboat.
To make the fleurons: Defrost and roll out a small piece of frozen puff pastry thinly and cut out circles with a small biscuit cutter. Using the same cutter, make crescent shapes and ovals from the circles. Bake on a dampened baking sheet in a hot oven (220°C/425°F or Gas Mark 7) for 10 to 12 minutes or until golden-brown, raising the oven temperature immediately after removing the partridges.

Partridges in piquant sauce; Oranges che yang; Crème Chantilly

Oranges che yang

Crème Chantilly makes a little cream go a long way. But the syrup from the can of mandarin oranges could be thickened with arrowroot and used as a sauce instead.

Metric	Imperial
1 × 311 g can mandarin oranges	1 × 11 oz can mandarin oranges
300 ml sweetened apple purée	½ pint sweetened apple purée
25 g preserved stem ginger, chopped	1 oz preserved stem ginger, chopped
1 × 5 ml spoon grated nutmeg	1 teaspoon grated nutmeg
1 × 15 ml spoon clear honey	1 tablespoon clear honey
2 × 5 ml spoons lemon juice	2 teaspoons lemon juice
2 × 15 ml spoons ginger syrup	2 tablespoons ginger syrup

Drain the mandarin segments from the syrup. Mix the fruit with the apple purée, chopped ginger, grated nutmeg, honey, lemon juice and ginger syrup.

Serve in small glasses with Crème Chantilly.

Crème Chantilly

Metric	Imperial
6 × 15 ml spoons double cream	6 tablespoons double cream
1 egg white	1 egg white
2 × 5 ml spoons caster sugar	2 teaspoons caster sugar
1 × 2.5 ml spoon vanilla essence	½ teaspoon vanilla essence

Whip the cream until it forms soft peaks. Wash and dry the beaters carefully then beat the egg white until stiff. Add the sugar and vanilla essence and continue beating until glossy. Lightly fold the meringue into the cream until well blended.

Dinner party for four

Menu

Buttered corn-on-the-cob

Kidneys in rich mustard sauce
served in rice rings

*Chinese leaf salad
or green salad

Banana and ginger dessert

*Individual cottage loaves with
English cheese platter:
Stilton, Double Gloucester and Somerset

Kidneys in rich mustard sauce

The richness of the mustard sauce blends well with delicately spiced rice and makes a pleasant change from cooked kidney served with potatoes.

Metric
8 lambs' kidneys
25 g butter
1 small onion, peeled and
    sliced
¼ kg mushrooms, sliced
Salt and freshly ground
    black pepper
1 × 15 ml spoon mild
    French mustard
4 × 15 ml spoons milk
4 × 15 ml spoons single
    cream

Imperial
8 lambs' kidneys
1 oz butter
1 small onion, peeled and
    sliced
½ lb mushrooms, sliced
Salt and freshly ground
    black pepper
1 tablespoon mild French
    mustard
4 tablespoons milk
4 tablespoons single cream
½ teaspoon grated nutmeg

1 × 2.5 ml spoon grated
    nutmeg
1 × 2.5 ml spoon freshly
    ground black pepper
225 g freshly cooked
    long-grain rice

½ teaspoon freshly ground
    black pepper
½ lb freshly cooked
    long-grain rice

Trim and slice the kidneys. Sauté the sliced kidneys in the butter in a large frying pan, remove them and keep warm.

Cook the sliced onion and mushrooms in the same pan, adding a little more butter if it has all been absorbed before the onion is soft. Season to taste, stir in the mustard, milk and cream mixed together. Add the kidneys and reheat slowly to boiling point, remove from the heat.

Fold the nutmeg and pepper into the hot cooked rice. Spoon heaps of rice on to 4 warm plates, make a dent in the centre of each heap with the back of a tablespoon. Fill with the kidney mixture. Garnish with chopped parsley.

142

Banana and ginger dessert

The banana topping turns an everyday blancmange into a luxurious party dessert, also delicious to serve at tea-time.

Metric	Imperial
1 × 33 g packet vanilla blancmange powder	1 × 1⅓ oz packet vanilla blancmange powder
2 × 15 ml spoons sugar	2 tablespoons sugar
600 ml milk	1 pint milk
100 g apricot jam	¼ lb apricot jam
4 bananas	4 bananas
75 g preserved stem ginger, finely chopped	3 oz preserved stem ginger, finely chopped
150 ml double cream	¼ pint double cream
1 × 5 ml spoon caster sugar	1 teaspoon caster sugar
1 × 2.5 ml spoon vanilla essence	½ teaspoon vanilla essence

Banana and ginger dessert; Kidneys in rich mustard sauce

Make up the vanilla blancmange using the sugar and milk, according to the directions on the packet. Pour into a shallow serving dish and allow to set.

Heat the jam and rub through a sieve. Peel the bananas, cut into halves lengthwise, then scoop out a little 'trough' down the centre of each half. Fill this with pieces of the very finely chopped ginger, reserving larger pieces for the decoration, and brush the sides of the bananas thickly with the jam. Arrange on the set blancmange.

Whip the cream, add the sugar and vanilla essence and pipe down the centres of the banana halves over the ginger. Decorate with the remaining pieces of ginger.

Dinner party for six

Menu

Melon

Grapefruit stuffed shoulder of lamb

Tiny roast potatoes

Chopped spinach

Apricot pancake layer

*Sherried custard sauce

Grapefruit stuffed shoulder of lamb

The meat of a lamb shoulder is often considered more succulent than that of the leg, but the shoulder is rather a difficult joint to carve. It is well worth boning out and roasting in this way. The bones can be used to make stock.

Metric	Imperial
1½ kg shoulder of lamb, boned	3 lb shoulder of lamb, boned
FOR THE STUFFING:	FOR THE STUFFING:
75 g fresh white breadcrumbs	3 oz fresh white breadcrumbs
2 × 5 ml spoons chopped parsley	2 teaspoons chopped parsley
Grated zest of 1 grapefruit	Grated zest of 1 grapefruit
50 g sultanas	2 oz sultanas
Salt and freshly ground black pepper	Salt and freshly ground black pepper
1 egg, beaten	1 egg, beaten
TO FINISH:	TO FINISH:
Grapefruit segments	Grapefruit segments
Parsley sprigs	Parsley sprigs

Spread out the boned shoulder, skin side down, on a board. Mix all the ingredients for the stuffing together. Cover the shoulder with the stuffing mixture and roll up neatly. Tie tightly with string in two places. Place in a roasting tin and put in the centre of a moderate oven (180°C/350°F or Gas Mark 4) for 25 minutes per ½ kg/1 lb of the stuffed weight. Remove the strings and serve on a warm platter surrounded by grapefruit segments placed alternately with parsley sprigs.

Serves 6

Apricot pancake layer

By heating briefly in the oven the finish of the pancake layer is delicately browned and crisp. If it has been prepared in advance of the party, you may require to leave the dish a few minutes longer in the oven to heat through.

Metric	Imperial
8 thin pancakes (see page 68)	8 thin pancakes (see page 68)
FOR THE FILLING:	FOR THE FILLING:
1 × 425 g can apricot halves	1 × 15 oz can apricot halves
2 × 5 ml spoons arrowroot	2 teaspoons arrowroot
3 × 15 ml spoons orange jelly marmalade	3 tablespoons orange jelly marmalade
1 × 15 ml spoon flaked almonds	1 tablespoon flaked almonds

Grapefruit stuffed shoulder of lamb; Apricot pancake layer

Fry the pancakes and keep them warm while you prepare the filling.

Drain the apricot halves and cut each one into 4 neat slices. Moisten the arrowroot with 1 × 15 ml spoon/ 1 tablespoon of the apricot syrup and put the remaining syrup in a saucepan with the marmalade. Stir over gentle heat until the marmalade has melted. Add the moistened arrowroot and bring to the boil, stirring constantly. Cook gently until the mixture thickens and clears, stirring all the time. Fold in the apricot slices.

Place one pancake on an ovenproof plate and cover with a little of the apricot filling. Continue in layers arranging a few good slices on top of the last pancake. Scatter with the flaked almonds and place in a moderate oven (180°C/350°F or Gas Mark 4) for about 15 minutes. Serve warm, cut into wedges. For special occasions, decorate with extra apricot slices.

Supper party for twelve

Menu

Pork and bean pot

Green salad

*Small cottage loaves and butter

French full red wine

Pork and bean pot

A good and inexpensive party dish. The quantity may be
halved if necessary to make a family meal.

Metric	Imperial
1 kg belly of pork	*2 lb belly of pork*
1 kg dried white beans, cannellini or haricot, soaked overnight	*2 lb dried white beans, cannellini or haricot, soaked overnight*
2 × 15 ml spoons olive or corn oil	*2 tablespoons olive or corn oil*
1 or 2 cloves of garlic, crushed	*1 or 2 cloves of garlic, crushed*
1 × 156 g can tomato purée	*1 × 5½ oz can tomato purée*
1 × 15 ml spoon soft brown sugar	*1 tablespoon soft brown sugar*
2 small bay leaves	*2 small bay leaves*
Salt and freshly ground black pepper	*Salt and freshly ground black pepper*
50 g fresh brown breadcrumbs	*2 oz fresh brown breadcrumbs*
15 g butter	*½ oz butter*

Remove any bones from the pork and cut the meat into
2.5 cm/1 inch squares. Drain the beans and rinse under
cold running water. Place in a large saucepan. Add the
bones from the pork and a little salt. Cover with cold water.
Bring to the boil and remove any scum with a slotted
draining spoon. Cover and simmer for 1 hour, or until
tender. Discard the bones.

Heat the oil in a sauté or large frying pan. Add the cubes
of pork and cook turning frequently until golden-brown.
Add the crushed garlic, tomato purée, sugar, bay leaves and
300 ml/½ pint of liquid from the beans. Season well and
simmer gently for 10 minutes.

Put a deep layer of drained beans in a large earthenware
casserole. Cover with the meat mixture and then the
remaining beans. Add sufficient bean stock just to cover.
Top with the brown breadcrumbs. Dot with a little butter
and bake uncovered in a warm oven (160°C/325°F or Gas
Mark 3) for 1½ to 2 hours.

Just before serving stir the crumb topping into the pork
and beans. Serve with a tossed green salad, fresh crusty
bread and an inexpensive red wine.

Supper party for four

Menu

Quick cassoulet

*Rembrandt's red cabbage

*Wholewheat popover rolls and butter

French red wine

Quick cassoulet

An unusual supper party dish that is guaranteed to satisfy the heartiest of appetites. The flavour resembles that of the famous French 'Cassoulet', without being nearly as rich.

Metric	Imperial
2 × 15 ml spoons vegetable oil	2 tablespoons vegetable oil
1 large onion, peeled and sliced	1 large onion, peeled and sliced
½ kg chipolata sausages	1 lb chipolata sausages
100 g streaky bacon, chopped	¼ lb streaky bacon, chopped
1 × 436 g can red kidney beans, drained	1 × 15 oz can red kidney beans, drained
150 ml beef stock	¼ pint beef stock
Salt and freshly ground black pepper	Salt and freshly ground black pepper
8 thin slices French bread	8 thin slices French bread
50 g Cheddar cheese, grated	2 oz Cheddar cheese, grated

Heat the oil in a frying pan. Add the onion and fry gently for 5 minutes. Add the chipolata sausages and the chopped bacon and fry gently for a further 5 minutes, turning the sausages occasionally.

Put the sausages, onion and bacon into a casserole. Add the drained red kidney beans, stock and seasoning to taste. Cover and cook in a moderate oven (180°C/350°F or Gas Mark 4) for 40 minutes. Remove the lid and cover the sausage and bean mixture with slices of French bread. Sprinkle with the grated cheese and return the cassoulet to the oven for a further 10 to 15 minutes, until the cheese bubbles.

147

Cocktail party food

Potato choux puffs

Cheesy cocktail biscuits

Stuffed fresh dates

Potato choux puffs

These small savoury puffs can either be served in place of potatoes with a main meal, or passed round as a hot party snack. Once cooked, they can be kept hot in a warm oven. A little grated Parmesan cheese can be added to the basic mixture before frying, if liked.

Metric	Imperial
1 quantity choux pastry (see page 116)	1 quantity choux pastry (see page 116)
½ kg potatoes, boiled and mashed	1 lb potatoes, boiled and mashed
Salt and freshly ground black pepper	Salt and freshly ground black pepper
Pinch of grated nutmeg	Pinch of grated nutmeg
Oil for deep frying	Oil for deep frying

Beat the choux pastry and mashed potato together in a bowl, season to taste and add the grated nutmeg. Put the potato and choux mixture into a piping bag fitted with a 1 cm / ½ inch plain nozzle.

Heat the oil in a deep-fat fryer or saucepan until it is hot enough to turn a stale bread cube golden in 45 seconds (185°C/360°F). Pipe out the choux mixture, cutting it into 1 cm / ½ inch lengths, and allowing them to drop gently into the hot oil. Fry for 1 to 2 minutes, until puffed and golden-brown. Drain on absorbent paper and serve hot.
Serves 6

Cheesy cocktail biscuits

Since you may expect a yield of about 24 finished biscuits, this is quite an economical recipe to make up and the flavour is delicious.

Metric	Imperial
175 g flour	6 oz flour
Pinch of paprika pepper	Pinch of paprika pepper
1 × 5 ml spoon dry mustard	1 teaspoon dry mustard
100 g butter	¼ lb butter
75 g Gouda cheese, grated	3 oz Gouda cheese, grated
2 × 5 ml spoons anchovy essence	2 teaspoons anchovy essence
1 egg, beaten	1 egg, beaten
FOR THE FILLING:	FOR THE FILLING:
50 g butter	2 oz butter
50 g Gouda cheese, grated	2 oz Gouda cheese, grated
4 anchovy fillets, finely chopped	4 anchovy fillets, finely chopped
FOR THE TOPPING:	FOR THE TOPPING:
25 g Gouda cheese, grated	1 oz Gouda cheese, grated

Sift the flour, paprika pepper and mustard together in a bowl and rub in the butter. Add the grated cheese and anchovy essence and bind with half the egg.

Roll out thinly on a floured board and cut out circles with a small round cutter.

Place the biscuits on baking sheets. Brush the tops of half the biscuits with the remaining egg and sprinkle on a little Gouda cheese before baking.

Bake in a fairly hot oven (200°C/400°F or Gas Mark 6) for 10 to 15 minutes until golden.

To make the filling:
Beat the butter and grated cheese together until soft, add the chopped anchovy fillets and use to sandwich the plain and cheese-topped biscuits together.

Stuffed fresh dates

Stone ½ kg/1 lb fresh dates, slitting with a sharp knife and removing the stone carefully. Divide a ¼ kg/½ lb block of marzipan into equal portions, the same number as the dates, and shape each piece into a long oval. Insert a roll of marzipan into each date to replace the stone. Arrange the stuffed dates on a platter or in paper sweet cases, in small dishes.

Cheesy cocktail biscuits; Stuffed fresh dates; Potato choux puffs

Children's party food

Fried potato shapes

Sausages in foil

Crispy chocolate pie

Fried potato shapes

Children love these fancy 'chips' for a party and they take little time and trouble to prepare. Nothing is wasted because the trimmings can be boiled and mashed for another meal.

Metric
1 kg large potatoes, peeled
Vegetable oil for frying

Imperial
2 lb large potatoes, peeled
Vegetable oil for frying

Cut the potatoes into even slices and stamp out shapes with tiny cocktail cutters. Rinse and drain very well.

Heat the oil in a deep-fat fryer or large saucepan until it is hot enough to turn a stale bread cube golden-brown in 30 seconds (190°C/375°F). Add the potato shapes and fry until crisp and golden-brown round the edges. Drain well on absorbent kitchen paper and serve hot with Sausages in foil.

Sausages in foil

These little sausage parcels will delight children and are ideal as a hot party dish.

Metric
24 cocktail sausages
2 × 15 ml spoons oil
1 large onion, peeled and
  thinly sliced
2 dessert apples, cored and
  chopped
Salt and freshly ground
  black pepper
25 g butter
25 g flour
300 ml cider

Imperial
24 cocktail sausages
2 tablespoons oil
1 large onion, peeled and
  thinly sliced
2 dessert apples, cored and
  chopped
Salt and freshly ground
  black pepper
1 oz butter
1 oz flour
½ pint cider

Cut 4 large squares of foil, turning up the edges, and place 6 cocktail sausages in the centre of each.

Heat the oil in a frying pan. Add the sliced onion and fry gently until soft. Add the chopped apple and cook gently for a further 3 minutes. Season to taste. Spoon the apple and onion mixture over the cocktail sausages on the foil squares. (If liked, fry the sausages for a few minutes first to brown them.)

Heat the butter in a small saucepan. Stir in the flour and cook for 1 minute. Gradually add the cider and bring to the boil, stirring constantly. Simmer until the sauce thickens. Spoon the cider sauce over the sausages, onion and apple.

Fold up the foil and pinch the edges well together to seal in the ingredients. Stand the foil parcels on a baking tray. Cook in a fairly hot oven (190°C/375°F or Gas Mark 5) for 30 minutes.

NOTE: Instead of cocktail sausages, you can use chipolatas; just twist each chipolata, to make 3 smaller sausages.

Crispy chocolate pie; Fried potato shapes; Sausages in foil

Crispy chocolate pie

Children really love the crisp chocolate case which is an ideal base to fill with a creamy dessert mixture, as suggested here, or with scoops of ice cream.

Metric	Imperial
25 g butter	*1 oz butter*
2 × 15 ml spoons golden syrup	*2 tablespoons golden syrup*
75 g plain chocolate, melted	*3 oz plain chocolate, melted*
100 g corn flakes	*¼ lb corn flakes*
300 ml Basic sweet white sauce (see page 32)	*½ pint Basic sweet white sauce (see page 32)*
150 ml black cherry yogurt	*¼ pint black cherry yogurt*
150 ml whipping cream	*¼ pint whipping cream*
Few small sweets to decorate	*Few small sweets to decorate*

Melt the butter and golden syrup together in a saucepan over gentle heat. Add the melted chocolate and the corn flakes and mix well until the flakes are well coated with the chocolate mixture. Spoon on to a 20 cm/8 inch pie plate, and press to the base and sides with a metal spoon, building up the edges slightly to make a lip around the outside. Chill well until firm.

Meanwhile, make up the white sauce and allow it to get cold. Stir in the yogurt.

Whip the cream until thick, reserve half for the decoration and fold the remainder into the yogurt mixture. Pour the filling into the pie case and chill until set. Serve decorated with rosettes of whipped cream and a few small sweets.

Instant strawberry and chocolate pie
If time is short, a packet of strawberry instant dessert made up with milk can be used as the filling. Alternatively, substitute strawberry yogurt for the black cherry yogurt.

Index

Acknowledgments

The publishers would like to thank the following individuals for their contributions to the photography in this book:

Bryce Attwell 2–3 front and back endpapers, 6–7 contents, 9 left and right, 10, 15 above left, above right, below left, below right and centre, 38 right, 79 above and below, 88–89, 90–91, 93 above, 94 right, 99 above, 100 left, 118–119, 126–127, 128–129, 131, 132–133, 134 above, 135, 136 left and right, 140–141, 148–149, 152–153, Melvin Grey 13, 16, 18, 29 above and below, 30 above left, 32 below, 32–33, 33 right, 34–35, 36 below, 37 above, 46–47, 49, 50 left, 51 left and right, 55 above, 58, 60–61, 76 left and right, 78, 80, 81, 82 left, 83 above, 84–85, 88 left, 89 right, 92, 93 below, 94 left, 96, 97, 98, 100 right, 101 left and right, 102 left, 102–103, 104 left, 105 left and right, 106–107, 107 below, 110 left and right, 111 below, 112 left and right, 113 left and right, 115 below, 116 above, 122, 123 above, 124 above, 125 left and right, 130 below and above, 134 below, 137 above, 138 left, 138–139; Paul Kemp 4–5 title spread, 11, 17, 21 above and below, 24–25, 30–31, 39, 40, 41 above, 42, 43 above, 52, 53 below and left, 54, 56–57, 59, 65, 66–67, 68–69, 70–71, 70, 71 below, 72–73, 74, 75, 77 left and right, 95 below, 108–109, 114–115, 116–117, 120 left, 120–121, 139 below right, 142–143, 144–145, 146, 147; John Lee 26 left and right, 27 left and right, 28 left, 38 left, 41 below, 45, 48, 62 left and right, 63, 86 above and below, 87, 118 above, 119 above.

The publishers would like to thank the following companies for the loan of accessories for photography:

Bejam Group Ltd; The Conran Shop; Craftsmen Potters' Association; Cucina; Elizabeth David; Divertimenti; Gered; Habitat; Jackson's of Piccadilly; Libertys; MegMell Galleries; David Mellor, ironmonger; Tilemart Ltd.; Worlds End Tiles.

WEIGHTS AND MEASURES

Imperial	US
2½ oz Allbran	1 cup
1 lb apples (diced)	4 cups
2 oz bacon, streaky	3 slices fatty bacon
2 oz bean sprouts	1 cup
4 oz black or redcurrants, blueberries	1 cup
4 oz breadcrumbs (fine dried)	1 cup
2 oz breadcrumbs (fresh soft), cake crumbs	1 cup
8 oz butter, margarine, lard, dripping	1 cup butter, margarine, shortening, drippings
3-4 oz button mushrooms	1 cup
8 oz cabbage (finely chopped)	3 cups
12 oz clear honey, golden syrup, molasses, black treacle	1 cup (1 lb =1⅓ cups) honey, maple syrup, molasses, black treacle
1 oz cooking chocolate	1 square baking chocolate
4½ oz cornflour	1 cup cornstarch
8 oz cottage, cream cheese	1 cup
¼ pint single, double cream	½ cup + 2 tablespoons (⅔ cup) light, heavy cream
2 oz curry powder	½ cup
3 oz desiccated coconut	1 cup shredded coconut
4 oz digestive biscuits (8 biscuits)	1 cup Graham crackers
7 oz dried chick peas, haricot beans	1 cup garbanzos, navy beans
4 oz flour, plain or self-raising	2 tablespoons all-purpose or self-rising flour
½ oz gelatine (1 tablespoon sets 2 cups liquid)	2 envelopes
3 oz preserved ginger (chopped)	⅓ cup
8 oz glacé cherries	1 cup candied cherries
3½ lbs gooseberries	9 cups
4 oz grated cheese, Cheddar type, Parmesan	1 cup
4 oz ground almonds	1 cup
7 oz long-grain rice	1 cup
4 oz macaroni, raw	1 cup
8 oz mashed potato	1 cup
8 oz minced raw meat	1 cup ground raw meat, firmly packed
4 oz nuts (chopped)	1 cup
2 oz onion (chopped)	½ cup
2 oz parsley (chopped)	1½ cups
6 oz pickled beetroot (chopped)	1 cup
6 oz peeled prawns	1 cup peeled shrimp
5-6 oz raisins, currants, sultanas (chopped), candied peel	1 cup (1 lb =3 cups)
5 oz raspberries	1 cup
3½ oz rolled oats	1 cup
8 oz sausagemeat	1 cup
5 oz strawberries, whole	1 cup
8 oz sugar, castor or granulated	1 cup, firmly packed
4 oz sugar, icing (sieved)	1 cup sifted confectioner's sugar
8 oz tomatoes (chopped)	1 cup
2¾ oz (smallest can) tomato purée	¼ cup
4 teaspoons dried yeast	4 teaspoons active dry yeast
¼ pint yoghurt	½ cup + 2 tablespoons (⅔ cup)

Liquid Measurements

20 fluid oz =1 Imperial pint	16 fluid oz =1 American pint
10 fluid oz =½ Imperial pint	8 fluid oz =1 American cup